MOTORING
FOR THE
MILLIONS

MOTORING
FOR THE
MILLIONS

IAN WARD

photography
Jasper Spencer-Smith

BLANDFORD PRESS
Poole   Dorset

First published in the UK 1981
Copyright © 1981 Blandford Press Ltd
Link House, West Street,
Poole, Dorset BH15 1LL

Distributed in the United States by
Sterling Publishing Co., Inc.,
2 Park Avenue, New York, N.Y. 10016.

British Library Cataloguing in Publication Data

Ward, Ian
   Motoring for the millions.
   1. Automobiles — History
   I. Title
   629.2′222′.09   TL15

ISBN 0 7137 1071 3

Filmset by Keyspools Ltd, Golborne, Lancs

Printed by Fakenham Press Limited,
Fakenham, Norfolk

CONTENTS

ACKNOWLEDGEMENTS

We are grateful to the following for kindly providing photographic material.

Autocar: page 89
André Citroën: page 127
BMC, Cowley: pages 62 (top), 101
British Leyland: pages 147, 150, 151
Neil Bruce: pages **28–9, 64–5**
Centro Storico Fiat: pages 78, 104
Gerard LeCompte, page 10
LNA Photos Ltd: page 116
Guy A. Morgan: page 62 (bottom)
National Motor Museum, Beaulieu: pages 14, 15, 18 (*bis*), 19 (*bis*), 21, 23, 24, 24–5, 25, 27, 30, 31, **32–3,** 35, 37, 44, 45, 46–7, 50 (*bis*), 51 (*bis*), 52, 56, 60, 61, 66, 67, 68, 71, 74 (*bis*), 75, 80, 84, 88, 90, 91, 95 (top and centre), 97, 100, 105, 107, 108, 123, 124, 126, 130, 132, 136, 141, 144, 145, 146, 152, 153
Nuffield Organisation, Cowley: pages 95 (bottom), 131
Renault U.K. Ltd: pages 156, 157
Volkswagen (GB) Ltd: pages 121, 122
Ian Ward: pages 34, 117, 137
Derek Watts: pages **5, 108–9**

(previous page)
One of the many versions of Panhard's Dyna model; this type was current during the 1950s.

INTRODUCTION

The idea that motoring could ever be for the millions is one that would have been dismissed as preposterous by all classes of society at the turn of the last century. Only the small, dedicated band of engineers and entrepreneurs who built and sold the seemingly frail and noisy machines would have accepted it as a sensible suggestion. It is true that once the motor car had gained a foot-hold among the horsedrawn fraternity it developed in leaps and bounds, but the horse had been almost undisputed king of the road for centuries before, and was not going to relinquish that title without a struggle.

The first attempts at replacing natural horse-power with the mechanical variety came as long ago as the sixteenth century, when various inventors, in several countries, began to wrestle with the sizable problem of how to propel a vehicle without the aid of animal power. Some outrageous contraptions were designed (this is perhaps a little too kind; many of them were no more than daydreams) and a few were actually built.

The wind was a favourite source of energy and this was harnessed – at least in the proposers' minds – by means of fans or turbines, by sails or by kites. Needless to say, none of these schemes turned out to be practicable, the wind on land being too unpredictable and too easily diverted. Clockwork power was also investigated, but the size of spring required to drive a full-scale carriage at a reasonable speed and over a useful distance was found to be excessively large. Winding such a spring was not quite like turning the key in one of the fine clocks of the period; several men – or perhaps even a horse – were needed for the task!

By the end of the seventeenth century, several notable scientists were coming to the conclusion that steam could be harnessed to provide a means of motive power. Experiments were carried out on several types of steam engine, from a simple turbine driven by a steam jet to a proper piston engine. A few inventors constructed models of their proposed vehicles, but it was not until 1769 that the first full-sized steam carriage was built. This was a massive goods wagon, or *fardier*, the brainchild of a French military engineer called Nicolas Cugnot. Despite state finance, this machine was not successful, being very crudely constructed and, as a result, almost uncontrollable; however, it did mark the beginning of a new era in road transport.

Most of the early steam vehicles were heavyweight coaches rather than cars, by any stretch of the imagination. Nevertheless, they did begin to make the horseless carriage seem as though it might be a practicality. It has to be remembered, however, that the state of the roads at that time was appalling and the ruts and pot-holes did much to encourage breakdowns. By comparison, the railways were ultra modern and highly efficient: the ride, although bone-jarring by today's standards, was velvet smooth compared with that of road carriages and the speed at which the trains could move was many times higher than the few miles per hour possible on the road.

It was not surprising then, that steam did not find a great deal of favour on the road at this time. The railways continued to have it their own way again until the middle of the nineteenth century, when roadgoing steamers began to be more practical. The carriages were not quite as massive as they had previously been and were thus capable of a considerably more respectable performance; at the same time the machinery was more highly refined and offered greater reliability than hitherto. Whereas some of the early contraptions made use of totally unsuitable mine engines or marine power units, the new generation favoured purpose-built motors with something like the necessary power and response.

Another major factor at this time was the number of engineers who were turning their attention towards steam power for the private carriage rather than the coach. Thomas Rickett led this renaissance by building a number of 'light' steam carriages (they were only light by previous standards; most of their space was occupied by a large boiler). Rickett and a number of contemporary constructors embarked on a series of proving trials in an effort to convince the public that steam power was not just acceptable, but was actually desirable and was here to stay. There were long-distance trips, there were attempts – and successes – at climbing steep hills and there were speed trials; there was also a large number of claims which could not be substantiated.

It is a measure of the success of the steamers

that the authorities in several countries, perhaps most famously in the UK, were panicked into legislating against the development of these devices; in most cases this was done by restricting the speed at which they could travel to somewhere around that of a horsedrawn carriage. It was, of course, hoped that this would remove any advantage which the steam vehicles had over the horse, but this did not work: people were prepared either to flout the law or live with it; few gave up.

As steam carriages became more sophisticated, so they also became more practical. The mechanical components began to disappear beneath seats or special cowlings and the devices began to look increasingly attractive to the ordinary member of the public, who was still suspicious of mechanical power. Amédée Bollée of Le Mans, in France, was a great steam pioneer and one of his vehicles, which he called *La Mancelle* (after his home town), and which he built in 1878, seems to have shown the way for the modern motor car, for its mechanical layout was very much along the lines that have become conventional today. Although it had a rear-mounted boiler, which seemed to form a base for many other mechanical parts, the three-cylinder engine was mounted under a front bonnet and it drove the rear wheels through a shaft and side chains. Being steam-driven, it did not require a clutch or a gearbox, both of which are almost universal in petrol-powered machines, but otherwise it set a precedent.

As good as steam was proving to be, it was obvious that it was not destined to provide a convenient means of motive power for the average private owner, who did not want to be bothered with waiting while the boiler heated up, not to mention lighting and stoking the fire and replenishing the water supply regularly. This was all very well for the railways, where a full-time fireman was employed on each train, or on public transport road vehicles, where the same arrangement was no problem, but if the ordinary man was to be enticed into the world of motoring he needed a simple and reliable machine which he could cope with on his own and which could be serviced and maintained quickly and cheaply. Garages, as such, were almost non-existent then, so it would be even better if the owner could feel confident of maintaining his own carriage.

Throughout the 1800s a considerable amount of work had been carried out on diverse kinds of internal combustion engine. These used equally diverse types of fuel, ranging from domestic coal gas, through paraffin to petroleum spirit. As with the early steam engines, many of these schemes were no more than pipe-dreams on the part of their proposers and others which did come to fruition failed to work at all or else needed a great deal of encouragement to struggle out of their dormant state for just a few seconds.

Gas engines were the first internal combustion units to prove effective and to be given practical applications. Barsanti and Matteucci in Italy were the first really to succeed, but they failed to capitalise on this and their motors were never taken up seriously. It was left to a Belgian, Jean-Joseph Etienne Lenoir, to produce a gas engine in any quantity. His unit ignited the fuel at low pressure and so an enormous capacity was needed in order to extract an extremely modest amount of power. Nevertheless, it did work and it was quite reliable and it did not take long for the engine to find many and varied applications in several countries. Lenoir did eventually construct a carriage to make use of his engine, but this carriage was very bulky and primitive and the power unit simply was not up to the job of propelling it.

After some years spent on producing a developed version of the Lenoir engine, mainly for static use, Nikolaus Otto and Eugen Langen realised that the free-piston (without connecting rods in the conventional sense), two-cycle engine offered little scope for further improvement. Otto then began work on a four-stroke engine powered by petrol and he made such a unit run quite well. Sensing that this was the route that gas engine development would now take, Otto attempted to patent the four-stroke cycle; indeed, he was successful in his attempt, and it took several years for the patent to be cancelled when it was shown that the theory of the cycle had been laid down some years previously by a Frenchman, Alphonse Beau de Rochas, in a patent document. Nevertheless, the brief Otto patent period forced many inventors to struggle with the task of finding alternatives to the 'Otto' engine, rather than perfecting the breed.

The forefront of engine development at this time was occupied by two Germans, Gottlieb Daimler, who had previously been employed by Otto, and Karl Benz. Both built petrol-powered four-stroke engines in the 1880s and both were soon testing them on the roads of Germany. The major difference between the approaches of the two men was that, while Benz installed his power unit in a purpose-built three-wheeler chassis, Daimler chose to adapt a horsedrawn carriage which he had commissioned in order to maintain secrecy. In fact Daimler's early trials were carried out with the new engine fitted to a boneshaker bicycle.

Development now followed quickly, with Benz concentrating more on automobile production than did Daimler, who was more interested in supplying his engines – and soon produced a 'high-speed', twin-cylinder unit – to other people. The first really practical Benz was the Viktoria of 1893, this being the company's first four-wheeler and having both respectable performance and reasonable reliability. Although this was probably the first motor car to be seriously offered to the public it did not find a great many takers and it was the Velo, which succeeded it in 1895, that caught on. Despite incredibly punitive laws relating to the motor vehicle – restricting it to 12 km/h (7 or 8 mph) on the open road and to half that in towns in parts of Germany – there were plenty of people willing to have a go, and the Velo was soon being manufactured on a kind of assembly line.

Daimler's engines were now finding their way into all sorts of foreign homes, manufacturing or marketing rights being acquired in several countries. Panhard and Levassor bought the French rights, passed them on to Peugeot and then proceeded to make their own car and engine, the latter bearing a distinct resemblance to the German unit. The British rights went to Frederick Simms, but he soon resold them to Harry Lawson, who saw the potential which they encompassed.

Despite all this activity, and despite an endless round of proving trials, such as the Paris–Rouen of 1894 and the British 1000-Miles Trial of 1900, motoring was still a hobby of the well-to-do. The car had been accepted as a *fait accompli* by the turn of the century and had certainly gained a reasonable level of respectability and reliability, but it was much too expensive for the average family. As is now so well known, limited output meant high costs and therefore high prices; unfortunately, however, the reverse also applied, so it was very difficult for the manufacturers actually to bring the costs and prices down.

De Dion, a company founded by Comte Albert de Dion, started the ball rolling by building very good single-cylinder engines, for their own use and for sale in massive numbers to other manufacturers, and making enough money out of this operation to enable them to construct their own small cars at a reasonable price. The idea certainly worked, for not only did just about every other make of car around the turn of the last century utilise a de Dion engine, but the de Dion cars were soon to be seen in what for the period were vast numbers. Even so, the company was still not properly geared up for economic production of its wares and in 1899 the price in Britain was by no means within the reach of the less well-off.

It was Henry Ford who was to become the champion of the common man. He started out by ignoring the infamous Selden patent, taken out in 1879, but carefully not published until 1895, by which time George Selden deemed that many companies had infringed it. Most manufacturers in the USA agreed to pay a licence fee to Selden in respect of every vehicle sold and formed the Association of Licensed Automobile Manufacturers (ALAM) to protect their interests. Ford decided that there was nothing in the Association which was of any use to him; he wanted to produce cars that were inexpensive enough for all and the lowest priced vehicle in the ALAM lists (and these prices were supposedly extra low) was much too costly for his tastes. In any case, he did not accept that Selden had patented the motor car, as was claimed.

Ford's policy was to make a car as simple as possible, while keeping it completely practical, thereby reducing costs to a minimum. He was then prepared to take something of a chance by pricing his cars on the assumption that they would sell in large quantities. He did not at first attempt to make a car for the people; he simply wanted to offer good value for money. As one new model followed another, however, he did manage to reduce the price.

In 1904, he was sued for infringement of the Selden patent, but he fought an expensive action which dragged on until 1911 and he finally defeated the ALAM. By this time, however, he could well afford the costs, as his company had made history with its legendary Model T, first visualised in 1907 and announced under 2 years later. The full story of this car for the masses is told later in the book, but the key to its success lay in the fact that Ford, in 1910, introduced a production line to the factory at Highland Park, near Detroit, which led to a full moving line by 1914.

More than any other motor vehicle, the Model T has stuck in motoring minds as the car for all. There is no doubt that it heralded the dawn of a new age and it caused all the competition to rethink its operation. Since then, there have been many popular cars which have been within reach of the average pocket. In Britain, Herbert Austin and William Morris led the cause for the impecunious motorist, in France we have Citroën and Renault to thank. In Germany, well, maybe Adolf Hitler did do something good. . . .

In this book we remember the classic popular motor cars – not necessarily the cheapest or the smallest – simply the machines which made possible *Motoring for the Millions*.

This 1900 example, with its artillery wheels, was the personal transport of Count de Dion.

DE DION SINGLE-CYLINDER CARS

One of the most famous names in the history of motoring must be that of Albert, Comte de Dion. Not only did his engines power almost every other vehicle in the pioneer days, but the novel and highly effective system of semi-independent rear suspension which bears his name is still in use today. Yet it was not really the Count who was responsible for either of these devices: they simply came out of his partnership with Georges Bouton and his brother-in-law, Monsieur Trépardoux, whose Christian name has been lost in the mists of time.

De Dion's interest in steam engines led him to buy a fine example of such a machine which he spied in a Paris shop window in 1881; more than that it led him to trace its builder, who turned out to be Bouton, and his assistant, Monsieur Trépardoux. De Dion found the two almost penniless, so it did not take much to persuade them to go into business with him to build steam cars. Trépardoux was the real steam expert and he was the brains behind a series of steam-powered vehicles which the trio turned out in the next few years. It was not surprising that he took umbrage when de Dion and Bouton moved on to design a new internal combustion engine in 1894, because they did this at the expense of further development in the field of steam power.

Trépardoux was upset enough to resign from the company, but by then he had already designed a steam wagon with what has since become known as de Dion suspension at the rear; the wheels were linked by a beam, but the final drive unit was mounted firmly on the chassis frame, driving the rear wheels by means of universally-jointed drive shafts.

After Trépardoux's departure, the steam vehicles were ignored, although they continued in production for several more years, and Bouton's first petrol engine appeared in 1895. This single-cylinder unit had a capacity of only 137cc and it was designed to run at low speed, as with the Benz units; however, it ran so badly that the bearings were quickly ruined and Bouton found that speeding it up to 2000 rpm or so ironed out all the problems. A spray-type carburettor fed mixture to the engine via an automatic inlet valve and trembler coil ignition set fire to the fuel.

The new engine was first fitted to a tricycle, in which it performed very well, and it was steadily enlarged to give an even better account of itself.

In 1898, concurrently with the tricycle, a primitive quadricycle was developed, still making use of the single-cylinder motor mounted at the rear, but this was very short-lived and in the following year the 402cc, $3\frac{1}{2}$ hp Model D *voiturette* was announced. This was a strange contraption, known as a *vis-à-vis*, in which the driver and one passenger sat facing another passenger in the front, but it was completely practical and performed well, with a maximum speed of nearly 32 km/h (20 mph).

This version of the engine was water-cooled (apart from the first few, which had air-cooled cylinder heads) and it was lubricated by splash, the oil being forced into the crankcase by a hand pump. Two forward speeds were fitted and these were selected by means of expanding clutches in constant-mesh gears, operated by a wheel mounted on the steering tiller shaft; there was no reverse gear on those early cars.

Initially the rear wheels were driven from the rear-mounted engine/transmission unit by means of a solid axle, with a differential but no suspension, but Bouton responded to pressure from the Count and fitted a de Dion layout, with three-quarter-elliptic leaf springs. At the front, the body rested on its beam axle by way of semi-elliptic springs and a rack-and-pinion steering unit kept the Ackermann layout in check. Braking depended on a foot-operated transmission brake (which also progressively reduced engine speed) and a brake band on the differential, initially operated by another pedal, but subsequently controlled by a hand lever. The chassis itself was of tubular-steel construction.

Although the de Dion was by no means cheap it sold in what were then vast numbers. By April of 1901, 1500 had been sold and the factory was turning out a phenomenal 200 cars each month. The *voiturette* was setting new standards for performance and passenger comfort and it did not take other manufacturers long to begin making close copies. This did not worry de Dion,

Overleaf. A 1901 de Dion voiturette, *with vis-à-vis seating. At this time the engine was still at the rear, but it produced* $4\frac{1}{2}$ *hp.*

however, as he was quite happy to sell them his own engine – in fact that power unit, in its various forms, sold incredibly well, 40 000 having been installed by 1904.

Engine power was steadily increased over the next year or two, through Models E, G, L and J, until, by 1902, power output was up to a more exciting 6 hp. Various styles of coachwork were by then available, ranging from a *vis-à-vis* to a delivery van; on the whole, however, coachwork was becoming more conventional, some models even being equipped with a dummy front bonnet. The 500cc, 4½ hp Model G was the first one to be equipped with a reverse gear, which was an epicyclic arrangement, operated by yet another pedal. Steering by this time was by wheel and a lever had replaced the gear wheel.

The dummy bonnet was symbolic, because in 1902 the company moved the engine into the front, leaving the transmission at the rear and

This Model G of 1901, with its dummy front bonnet, may have had reverse gear, but it was none the more reliable for it.

joining the two by means of a short shaft. The first, and the most popular, of these cars was the 700cc 6 hp model in two-seat form, known as the Populaire. This weighed 305 kg (6 cwt) and it managed a daring 48 km/h (30 mph); more importantly it sold in vast numbers. Later in the year, a third gear was added to the box of the new 8 hp Model K, with a 942cc engine and styling reminiscent of the contemporary Renault.

Around this time, different models abounded, but they all had the same basic format, with either 6 hp or 8 hp engines. Demand was still enormous and the factory at Puteaux was employing 1300 workers in 1904. The next important development was the introduction of a three-speed crash gearbox in 1905 on the 8 hp model of that year. There was nothing wrong with the old unit, but the current trend was towards the sliding-pinion unit, so de Dion obeyed. At the same time, the tubular chassis was replaced by a pressed-steel item, which seemed to work just as well.

Although this was in 1905, a new tubular car emerged in 1906, complete with the old gearbox and known as the AL. This, the last such car, was also propelled by the 942cc, 8 hp unit, but it was short-lived, a new twin-cylinder model, as well as a four, now being in the catalogue. To cope with demand for all these cars, the payroll now amounted to around 3000 and it was still possible to obtain all sorts of different body styles (one of the most popular was the doctor's coupé, which really did sell well within the medical profession).

Changes were fewer after this, but sales were maintained at high levels for several more years. The automatic inlet valve was replaced by a mechanical version in 1907 and soon after magneto ignition was substituted for the some-times temperamental trembler coil. Power output went up again to 12 hp in 1909, with a capacity increase to 1020cc, but it was probably a mistake to drop the de Dion rear axle in 1911, as demand fell off after that to the extent that the series, a fine example to the whole of the industry, was finally killed altogether in 1913. Although it built a V8, which was probably the first of its kind, the company never really built as original a car as the single-cylinder model again and it drifted into relative obscurity before its final demise in 1932.

In 1902, the engine was finally moved to the front for the 6 hp Populaire and later in the year this Model K appeared, with a third gear.

FORD MODEL T

In the early part of this century, motoring was very much a luxury, something to be enjoyed only by the well-to-do. However, there were a few pioneer manufacturers who recognised a need for cheaper cars and the leader among these was the American, Henry Ford. In 1906, he replaced his Model F, a primitive twin-cylinder machine, with a new four-cylinder-engined Model N, which was an altogether better vehicle, but which amazingly sold for substantially less.

This was still not good enough for Henry Ford, however; the Model N, despite its fairly refined engine, was a very basic motor car – which was why it was so cheap. Ford wanted to build a car which would be cheap enough for anyone who could afford to buy a horse and carriage and which, more importantly, would sport a specification comprehensive enough to attract those people and inspire their confidence in the machine. The price would be held down by virtue of the car's, hopefully, massive sales.

Henry Ford's ideas were translated into drawings – on a blackboard – by an engineer, Joseph Galamb, and then prototypes were built. The use of tough steels enabled the car to be strong yet light, while the side-valve, four-cylinder, 2892cc engine produced little power but had a respectable torque figure which endowed the car with good hill-climbing abilities. The new car was given the code letter T because other letters between N and T had been allocated to developments of the Model N.

When Ford announced his new car in October 1908, he announced, too, his intention for this to be his company's only product in the foreseeable future; so confident was he that the Model T would satisfy an enormous demand that he saw no reason to offer any alternative models. As motoring legend now tells us, of course, he was absolutely correct in his judgement, setting the style for many others.

When the price of the T was announced Ford dealers were so staggered that a car of this standard could be sold so cheaply that they hid the advance publicity material from the public lest they be left holding stocks of the T's markedly more primitive predecessors. Everything about the car was simple but effective. The chassis was outwardly very crude, but was really quite strong, while the transverse leaf spring suspension gave a remarkably good ride over rough roads, particularly at speeds below about 48 km/h (30 mph). In those days of non-synchromesh gearboxes the two-forward-speed epicyclic gearbox fitted to the 'Tin Lizzie' – as it affectionately became known – was an undoubted joy to use, even if its foot pedal operation was somewhat eccentric.

The engine's plentiful torque meant that a third forward gear was unnecessary, although a little more power than the standard 20 bhp would have been useful. This power lack was due to restrictions in the manifolds and ports, so it could easily have been overcome, but it never was. The trembler coil ignition was troublesome, having to be finely adjusted to make starting easy (stories have been told of Ts whose ignition has been left on, so that a small vibration has caused a spark and fired any cylinder with a piston at the top of its compression stroke, thus self-starting the engine).

Bodywork styles were numerous during the Model T's life, ranging from a two-seat tourer to a five-seat saloon. Initially, however, all coachwork was of the open variety and weather protection was minimal. With a top speed of around 72 km/h (45 mph) and a fuel consumption of up to 9.4 l/100 km (30 mpg), the 'Tin Lizzie' was very advanced and there was little doubt in any mind that she would catch on.

Initially, sales were slow compared with those of the Model N, but they soon began to pick up and, in 1909, more than 80 000 cars were sold. Although Ford is widely held to have pioneered mass production with the Model T, this is not wholly true: mass production techniques were already being employed in other industries and it was the moving line, in which the cars are moved to the workers for each job to be completed, that he introduced. In any case, it was not until the company moved to Highland Park, north-west of Detroit, in 1910, that Ford even began to install a production line as such. It was 1914 before mass production truly arrived; by then it took only 1½ hours to assemble each car.

1914, when this four-seat tourer was built, saw the introduction of Ford's famous 'black only' policy, which was to last until 1925.

A black radiator surrounded was standardised in 1917 and the doctor's coupé body style, as on this 1918 Model T, was one of the most popular and attractive.

A central door, as in this 1921 sedan, was intended to make access to both front and back as easy as possible.

The Model T continued unchanged after World War 1 and prices were slashed to help sales. This four-seat tourer was built in 1919.

By 1927, when the Model T was finally dropped, it was still basically the same car as it had been 10 years earlier.

All manners of body style appeared on the Model T chassis; this 1919 Jobmaster landaulette is one of the rarer examples.

By this time, sales had rocketed and, in 1915, the 1 millionth Model T left the line. The car was also being produced at Ford factories in other countries, principally Trafford Park near Manchester in Great Britain and the price was steadily coming down. The famous phrase 'Any colour as long as it's black' is said to have been Henry Ford's description of the range of hues offered; so it was, but this was in fact only true of the cars manufactured from 1914 to 1925, a black radiator surround being standardised in 1917.

All sorts of Model T variants were marketed, from farm tractors to ambulances, and from fire engines to 1-ton trucks. During World War 1, thousands of Ts were supplied to the Allies; indeed only the T and the Rolls-Royce Silver Ghost could cope with the conditions in the Mesopotamian desert, where large numbers of Fords were deployed.

After the war, taxes began to rise and loans became more expensive, so car sales fell. Henry Ford's answer to this was to slash his prices, so much so that he was actually losing money on each car (although the extras sold with every T brought the profit back). This caused consternation among Ford's rivals, who were forced to follow suit and in many cases became bankrupt. However, T sales thrived again, to the extent that 1923 was the car's best year, an incredible 2 million cars being built.

Strangely, this figure represented a very sharp peak on a graph, for from this point on sales plummeted until, when this legendary machine was finally killed by its 'father' in 1927, only a dribble of Model Ts was leaving the showrooms. Henry Ford, for all his foresight in dreaming up this marketing masterpiece, was a died-in-the-wool reactionary and he refused to believe that his pride and joy was becoming obsolete. Throughout its life, the major changes were only to bodywork; under the skin the T, in 1927, was still the same as the car which had won the world's hearts in 1908. It may have had an electric starter and proper lights, but it still had primitive two-wheel-and-transmission brakes and it was by no means reliable (although part of its attraction was that it was very easy to service and repair).

By the time the end came, in May 1927, over 15 million Model T Fords had left the various factories around the world – and this remained a record until the Volkswagen 'Beetle' overtook it many years later. Henry Ford killed the car so suddenly that he had not readied a replacement for the market, perhaps one of the drawbacks of a one-model policy. The factory at Highland Park stood idle for 6 months before the elegant new Model A emerged.

The Model T had probably lasted 2 or 3 years longer than it should have, in the face of more modern opposition, but it had served motorists well for 19 years and about three-quarters of the cars sold since 1908 were still in use in 1927 – a fitting tribute indeed.

MORRIS 'BULLNOSE' COWLEY AND OXFORD

William Morris formed several unprofitable partnerships during his early career, but it was not very long before he decided that the only way to do what he wanted was to work alone. In 1910 he calculated that there was scope for a fairly simple car, with consequent low running and repair costs and he further reckoned that such a car would sell in large numbers. Morris's approach to the manufacture of this machine was totally opposed to that of Henry Ford with his Model T.

Whereas Ford's method was to build as much of the car as he possibly could, Morris took the converse route and assembled his new Morris Oxford from components supplied almost entirely from outside his small factory at Cowley, near Oxford, Great Britain. The engine came from White & Poppe, complete with a gearbox, and the other parts came from far and wide.

This Oxford, which was announced in March 1913, was a great success, but it was too small to be fitted with anything other than a two-seater body. By March 1917, when production ceased, 1475 examples had been turned out, but Morris had by then introduced this car's much more famous successor. He had originally planned to introduce a stretched version of the Oxford, with a new White & Poppe engine, but he found that this would be prohibitively expensive, even compared with American imports.

The first Morris to bear the Oxford name was this little two-seater, manufactured between 1913 and 1917.

In 1923, the Oxford grew into a larger version of the Cowley. This is a rare all-weather body of 1924.

By 1924 the Cowley had undergone a variety of changes, including the acquisition of suspension dampers. This is a four-seat open tourer.

He made an exploratory trip to the USA to find out just how the Americans could put cars together so cheaply. Accompanied by Hans Landstad, chief draughtsman of White & Poppe, he obtained the plans for a four-cylinder, 1500cc engine and quotes for vast numbers of varied supplies. On his return, he asked White & Poppe to work out a price for an engine such as this, but the company couldn't begin to approach the staggeringly low figure asked by the Continental Manufacturing Company of Detroit. The two returned to America to place orders, and on their way they designed a four-seater family car around the components for which they had received quotes during their last visit. When they arrived, they arranged for the supply of enough parts to make 3000 Cowleys, as the new car was to be called.

Sadly, World War 1 intervened and Continental cabled Morris to ask if he wanted to cancel

The original Oxford was not a bad car, but it was too small for anything larger than a two-seat body. This is a 1915 coupé.

the order; however, his answer was to ask for greater haste. He thus received the first, trial, engine by the end of 1914 and was able to show the car to the Press in April 1915. Landstad had stayed on to learn the ways of the American motor industry and help Continental with production of the Red Seal engine for Morris. When all was well, he returned to White & Poppe, but it was not long before he joined Morris full-time.

The new Cowley was an altogether far better car than the Oxford, having such luxuries as a detachable cylinder head and full electric lighting with a dynamo (in place of acetylene lamps). In addition to this, and the facts that the Cowley could take a two-seat or four-seat body and was generally bigger than its sister, it was a little cheaper.

The four-cylinder engine had a capacity of 1495cc and breathed through side valves and a horizontal Zenith carburettor. Magneto ignition fired the engine, which was water-cooled by means of a fan-assisted thermo-syphon system. Strangely, this was one of the first engines to make use of a dipstick to show oil level. A two-plate-dry-clutch fed the power to a three-speed-

and-reverse gearbox in unit with the engine and a propeller shaft running in a torque tube completed the journey to the rear axle, itself unusual in that it was of lightweight, yet sturdy, welded-pressed-steel construction with a spiral-bevel crown wheel-and-pinion set (almost unheard of in those days of straight-cut gears).

Suspension was by means of three-quarter-elliptic springs at the rear and half-elliptic ones at the front. A lack of caster on the front end meant that the steering, which was through a worm-and-spur box, had no self-centring effect. Brakes were fitted to the rear only, except in the later models, but these were quite effective, and dampers were not introduced until 1923.

Although the price was very reasonable, this was by no means a 'cheap' car, being equipped with such luxuries as leather upholstery, real mahogany trim and a separate door for the driver.

Many of the metal parts were smartly nickel-plated and the standard colour for the coachwork was a pleasing chocolate brown. The 'Bullnose' nickname, never an official title, came from the strange bulbous radiator utilised.

It was September of 1915 before the Cowley became available to the public and a government import duty of $33\frac{1}{3}$ per cent pushed up the price almost immediately. Morris ran into various problems quickly: nearly half the 3000 engines went to the bottom of the Atlantic, so that there was a surplus of most chassis components, and then, in March 1916, the government introduced a total ban on component imports – unless they were for commercial vehicle use. The Morris answer to the second problem was to bring out a

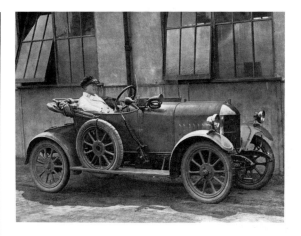

The two-door body was a mainstay of Cowley production throughout its life and was the only style available immediately after the War.

Cowley delivery van, while the loss of the engines did not make itself felt for some considerable time.

Most Cowleys were equipped with the standard two-seat or four-seat body, but quite a large number of chassis were sold for special bodies to be fitted. 'Official' coupé and cabriolet bodies were listed in 1916 and 1918 respectively, but very few of these were sold.

Unlike many of Britain's motor manufacturers, Morris managed to continue building cars throughout World War 1, although this was hampered more and more by munitions production during the latter half of the conflict. All told, 1133 Cowleys were produced in the war years and this gave the company a sound base from which to work in post-war times. This was fortunate, because the post-war boom brought to a head the problem of the lack of engines. For the first time, Morris had to cut production when he could have sold far more cars and his headache was aggravated by Continental deciding that they no longer wanted to produce the Red Seal engine (although the government restrictions were still in force in any case). Luckily he owned the rights to the motor and the French Hotchkiss company, who had an idle factory in Coventry, stepped in to build a Red Seal copy. The first engine was

A four-door saloon version of the 1925 Oxford.

finished in July 1919 and the Cowley was back in production by September.

The new Cowley was much the same as the old; one problem, that of a leaky rear crankshaft oil seal bringing about clutch slip, was ingeniously circumvented by the adoption of a cork clutch running permanently in an oil bath, motor cycle fashion. Otherwise changes were very few, except that the Oxford name reappeared on the de luxe version of the car, which retained the specification of the Continental Cowley, while its sister went without leather seats, full instrumentation or a dynamotor (for starting *and* charging).

One of Morris's big mistakes was to increase the price of the cars; by late 1920 the price of the two-seater had risen amazingly and was simply too much for the market. At the end of the year, the bubble burst and sales slumped to almost nothing. Morris's answer was completely unexpected: he knocked about 20 per cent off the price of the four-seater and a little less off its little sister and this had exactly the desired effect. The announcement was made in early February and sales leaped from sixty-eight in January to 244 during the next month. Nor did Morris stop there: just as the rest of the industry recovered from the shock and cut prices by an average of 17 per cent for the 1921 Motor Show, the price of

the 'Bullnose' came down again. The horsepower tax of 1921 gave the car an advantage over some rivals, despite a price discrepancy, as it had a low rating at 12 hp compared, say, with the Model T Ford at 22 hp. 1923 saw the Oxford grow to be a bigger car than the Cowley, in length and engine size, but it retained its 'Bullnose' appearance.

From 1921 until the end, Morris reduced prices regularly. What is more, the specification was improved: a starter was fitted, as were better instruments and balloon tyres. In 1921–22, a short run of pretty aluminium-bodied sports cars was produced, 107 in all, and during other years various slight body changes took place. 1926 saw rod-operated four-wheel brakes fitted at last, along with a new front axle giving the steering some self-centring. However, despite the very low price, the car had been allowed to survive too long and sales dropped alarmingly. In September of that year, the 'Bullnose' was finally replaced by a flat-radiatored car, albeit still closely based on the original.

In its long and varied career, the 'Bullnose' reached 154 000 purchasers and rightly found a place in motoring history. Perhaps its main claim to fame ought to be that the Cowley displaced the ubiquitous Model T as Britain's best-selling car, a remarkable feat indeed.

DODGE 3½ LITRE

The two Dodge brothers, John, the elder by 4 years, and Horace were inseparable; they did everything together and they spent a good deal of their time fighting – they did not seem to mind whether it was someone else or each other. They were hardly educated, but they had some sort of sixth sense, which they employed to the full in getting into business together. They had intuition and business acumen in plenty, together with a kind of low cunning, which enabled them to make the right moves and the right decisions.

After a spell working together for other people, they set up the Evans and Dodge Bicycle Company, in Ontario, Canada, to build their own design of cycle. This was soon taken over, however, so the pair returned to Detroit, where they established a highly efficient machine shop, whose reputation for precise work and cleanliness soon spread far and wide. It was not long before the company was asked to manufacture components for the new but expanding motor industry and, by 1903, several companies were competing for the Dodge concern's services.

After weighing up all the offers, the brothers decided to accept Ford's order for chassis and agreed in February to build 650 such chassis for the first batch of Ford cars. This work went so well that, before long, the Dodge company was doing very little other than Ford work. The whole set-up seemed almost too good to be true: John was made a director – and ultimately Vice-President – of Ford and the pair were given 350 shares each. However, John and Horace realised, with their good business sense, that the Ford deal

In 1916, when this centre-door saloon was made, the wheelbase was lengthened and the brakes were improved.

could fold overnight and leave them with nothing. Furthermore, they were not being paid a great deal for their work.

By 1913, the two had made a decision to build their own cars, so that they would only be in the hands of the customers, whom it was up to them to satisfy. They had plenty of money. Although John resigned his seat on the Ford board in August of 1913, they retained their shares, which now amounted to 4000, and these amassed them over $1 million per year in dividends; on top of this, they had property worth over $30 million.

Rather than make use of an existing factory, which in any case they would have to convert extensively for car manufacture, the brothers decided to purpose-build a new plant on a piece of land at Hamtramck which they had owned since 1910. Here they worked on their new machine and built the first production car on 14 October 1914 – quite a remarkable feat, helped not a little by the knowledge which they had gained from their Ford work. They launched the car on the people in November, and it received a rapturous welcome from a public eager for an alternative to the Model T.

In specification, the Dodge was entirely conventional in almost all respects. The engine was a side-valve, four-cylinder, monobloc unit, with a capacity of 3.5 litres and a power output of 25 bhp. The most interesting feature about this water-cooled unit was that it was equipped with a 12-volt electrical system featuring a North-East dynastart (a piece of machinery which served the dual purpose of starting the engine and charging the battery). This ingenious device was set up in such a way that, should the engine stop with the ignition turned on, the dynastart would automatically switch into its starting mode and revitalise the motor. Despite this advanced feature, ignition relied on a magneto.

A cone clutch provided a link between the front-mounted engine and a sliding-pinion three-speed gearbox, mounted in unit with the motor. Although the gearbox itself was of conventional construction, the change was arranged so that the central lever operated 'back to

One of the earliest examples of the Dodge 3½ litre, a two-door open tourer model constructed in 1915.

A 1918 four-door open tourer version of the Dodge $3\frac{1}{2}$, with precious little weather protection.

front', the two upper ratios being on the left-hand side of the gate. A torque tube housed the propeller shaft and joined the gearbox to the rear axle, which drove the rear wheels by courtesy of a spiral-bevel final-drive unit.

Suspension for the beam front axle and the live rear axle was by means of semi-elliptic leaf springs all round and brakes were provided only on the rear wheels. The first cars built were four-seat tourers, but it was not long before several other body styles joined the range. For the price the Dodge represented a very modest investment and extremely good value for money.

The success of the new machine was assisted by the fact that the work of the Dodge brothers was well known in the trade through the company's association with Ford. It was not long before there were 22000 dealers around the USA who were all competing for Dodge agencies. Fortunately, mass production got under way

very rapidly and, by the end of 1915, a total of 45000 cars had left the factory; more importantly, this meant that Dodge was only behind Ford and Willys-Overland in the sales league – Dodge had well and truly arrived.

Although the car did not really need publicity, it must have been helped along when General Pershing ordered 250 Dodges to serve as staff cars in his campaign against Pancho Villa, a notorious Mexican bandit of the time; not only this, but Villa himself made the Dodge his official car, although this does not seem to have helped him much, as he was killed in it in 1923. The success of Pershing's staff cars led to the model's adoption as official US Army transport.

Changes to the Dodge were remarkably few

during a life of 14 years, although body styling was updated along the way. 1916 saw the introduction of a multi-disc clutch, together with larger brake drums, a lengthened wheelbase and the option of all-steel bodywork for the tourer, manufactured by the Budd company of Philadelphia, which had already made a name for itself in this field (a few all-steel saloons were also made).

Perhaps the most important event of 1916 was that the brothers brought a law suit against Henry Ford and his company, because the great man had refused to pay any further dividends to shareholders. They won their action, but the end result was that Ford bought out them and all the other shareholders for $106 million, $25 million of which actually went to the Dodges. This had been Ford's aim all along, for it meant that he now had total control over his rapidly growing empire. Despite the legal action, however, the Dodges and Henry Ford remained on very good terms throughout their lives.

Sadly, John and Horace did not live much longer to enjoy their fortune – and their fame. They both contracted pneumonia and died only months apart; their widows inherited ownership of the company, but the day-to-day running of it was put in the hands of a man called Frederick Haynes.

Meanwhile, the Dependable Dodge, as the brothers had christened it, went from strength to strength. By 1920, it was second only to the Model T Ford in the sales league, although it was still the only car manufactured by Dodge. That year, with the company turning out over 600 cars a day, saw some restyling, the body having a slanted windscreen and being generally more streamlined. In 1923, stop lamps and an anti-theft gearbox lock became standard and by 1924 production had again increased to 1000 cars a day. It was in 1924 that the 1 millionth Dodge left the line at Hamtramck and demand showed no signs of decreasing.

Unfortunately, the company was not as suc-

By 1925, Budd all-steel bodywork was common on the Dodge, but the car was coming towards the end of its life.

cessful as its product; the concern was not being run as well as it had been when the brothers were alive. In 1925, it was taken over by a firm of New York bankers, who allowed it to continue substantially unchanged. The 3.5 continued as the sole bearer of the Dodge standard, the back-to-front gearchange and the 12-volt electrics being dropped in 1926; it seems strange that 6 volts were more popular than 12 in those days – such a system would be ridiculed if used today.

1927 saw the company in trouble once more, and this time it was sold to Chrysler, after a considerable amount of argument (Chrysler later claimed it was the best move he had ever made). By now the 3.5's power output had been increased to 40 bhp and it had the luxury of four-wheel brakes, but a new six-cylinder unit appeared in 1927 and the last was sold a few months later, just after the Chrysler take-over had been completed in July 1928. Over 1½ million 3.5-litre Dodges had by then found happy owners.

CITROËN TYPE A

André Citroën took over the helm of the ailing Mors concern in 1908 and succeeded, at least temporarily, in bringing it back to profitability. However, he was a man of foresight and in 1913 he set up his own gear-making concern, to produce solely the herringbone-toothed cogs which he had previously introduced on Mors final drive units and on which he held a patent. These had the advantage over more conventional items of having the silence of diagonally-cut gears and almost the efficiency of straight-cut teeth.

In 1915, Citroën decided to go into car production on his own behalf and he arranged for a factory to be built on waste land at the Quai de Javel in Paris (now known as the Quai André Citroën). Using knowledge that he had gained during visits to the Ford factory in the USA, Citroën made sure that he had all the latest mass production equipment installed from the word go. By 1917, the factory was finished and Citroën, together with the former Le Zèbre designer, Jules Salomon, set about planning two new cars. One of these was a luxury machine with a 4-litre, sleeve-valve engine and the other was a smaller car, with a 1.3-litre, four-cylinder unit. The large vehicle was subsequently taken up by Voisin, but the other became the first Citroën, when it was produced on 28 May 1919. Not only was this the first machine to bear the Citroën name; it was also the first motor car to be mass produced in Europe.

The 1327cc engine of the Type A, as the car was known, was rated at 10 hp. It was an in-line four, with two main bearings, and the side-mounted valves were operated directly by a single block-mounted camshaft. A cone clutch and a three-speed gearbox, without synchromesh, were mounted in unit with the engine at the front of the car; a double-jointed propeller shaft, in this case not running in a torque tube, was utilised to transmit the power from there to the live rear axle, via a spiral-bevel final drive unit.

Suspension was by quarter-elliptic leaf springs all round, leading at the front and trailing at the

In 1921, the Type B2, with 1½-litre engine, supplemented the similar A in the range.

An English family outing in one of the last Type As, a 1922 10.4 hp tourer.

rear, but no dampers of any sort were offered, so the ride was a little bouncy. The front axle took the form of a forged beam. Braking was taken care of by foot pedal and hand lever, but the foot brake acted only on a transmission drum, while the hand brake worked two drums in the rear wheels.

The Type A was unusual in more ways than simply being mass produced, for it came with full electrical equipment and an almost unheard of electric starter. What is more, it left the production line absolutely complete, unlike some other products which had to be taken in chassis form to coachbuilders to have bodywork added. Five body styles were advertised: three and four-seat open tourers, a three-seat saloon, a *coupé-de-ville* and a van; whichever of these was selected was fitted at the factory, so that the car was ready to be driven away by the purchaser.

The Type A was announced before the first car had been built and the reaction from the public

The Type A was the first car to bear the Citroën name. This 1919 example was one of the earliest.

was astonishing. Admittedly the price was considerably lower than that of any rival, but without anyone having seen the car, orders began to pour in. In the advertising for the Type A, Citroën announced that the car was: 'For those who consider that a motor car is an asset in one's work as well as one's leisure', and the direct result of that was that within 2 weeks 16 000 orders had been received – still before the car had been shown.

In all, 30 000 orders were placed before production started and Citroën's multitude of critics had to swallow their words. André had probably well deserved a considerable amount of scepticism, because he stated early on that he intended to be producing 100 cars per day very soon; this was an astonishing number for the period, in Europe, but by 1924 that figure had in fact been exceeded by a factor of two. Citroën was a superb publicist, not relying solely on straightforward advertising to bring sales. At the Paris Motor Show later in 1919, he cleverly arranged for 50 of his Type A models to be available for potential customers to take for demonstration drives; he also organised visits to the factory for the general public and in 1920 he replaced the entire Paris taxi fleet at a stroke with his own cars. His schemes were endless, culminating in the company renting the entirety of the Eiffel Tower's four sides between 1925 and 1934 to advertise the Citroën name in letters 30 m (100 ft) high, formed from 250 000 electric light bulbs.

When the waiting public finally saw and tried the Type A, it was by no means disappointed, for here was a totally practical 10 hp car at a price many people could easily afford. The fact that the machine weighed only 450 kg (just under 9 cwt) in chassis form must have helped the performance considerably, because it had a maximum speed of 64 km/h (40 mph) from its actual output of 18 bhp and, more importantly, a remarkable fuel consumption of nearly 7 l/100 km (40 mpg) and a very good, for the time, oil consumption of about 112 km/l (35 miles to the pint) – indicating perhaps that the engine was not highly stressed.

Although so many orders had been placed before the car's appearance, subsequent sales must have been aided by a strike at the Renault factory in June, just as the first cars were reaching customers. Citroën made the most of this and sales continued to boom. Unlike several other major manufacturers, Citroën very quickly set up a large network of agents in 1919, totalling 200 by the end of the year. This meant that, on the rare occasion when the Type A let its owner down, there was usually an authorised dealer in the vicinity to deal with the problem. A considerable number of cars were exported to Great Britain and other countries and, over the years that followed, Citroën set up subsidiaries in all the major countries where their cars were sold, including one in Hammersmith, London.

In 1921, the year in which around 10 000 Type As were made, the original model was joined in the range by a modified version known as the Type B2. This was very similar to the A, but was slightly bigger, with a 1.5-litre version of the engine. A sports version, known as the Caddy, was also derived from the A in that year and this had a maximum speed of nearly 97 km/h (60 mph).

The Type A soldiered on into 1922, still selling remarkably well, but it was dropped in that year, when the famous 5CV, irreverently known as the 'Citroën Pressé' due to its almost invariable yellow colour, was announced.

FIAT 501

Despite being Italy's largest car manu-facturer, Fiat surprisingly had built nothing in large quantities by the time the 1920s were approaching. Even the popular Zero managed to find a place in only just over 2000 homes during its short life between 1911 and 1915. In 1918, however, Giovanni Agnelli, the founder and proprietor of Fiat (or more correctly FIAT, since the letters were initials representing Fabbrica Italiana Automobili Torino), decided to change all that, by building a new factory in Turin, complete with its own rooftop test track, and installing a moving production line for the manufacture of his new economy car, the 501.

Carlo Cavalli, who was responsible for the design of the 501, was a lawyer by profession; not entirely happy in his work, he had joined Fiat in 1905 as a draughtsman. Most of his work was concentrated on the highly successful Fiat racers in the early part of his career and by the time he started work on the 501, he had risen from the ranks in recognition of his achievement; in 1919, when his new brainchild went on sale for the first time, he was Technical Director.

Although the 501 was a small economy car, it was by no means a baby when compared with other miniature's, such as Peugeot's Quadrilette or the yet-to-come Austin Seven. This honour was left to the type 500, designed jointly by Cavalli and Guido Fornaca and announced alongside the 501 in 1918. Demand for the 501, however, was such that there seemed little point in producing the 500, which would in any case have stretched the factory's capacity; another underlying influence here was that Agnelli was not convinced that the world was yet ready for a tiny car such as the 500 – and he may well have been right.

The Fiat 501 – or 'Lawyer's Fiat', as it was colloquially known, after the previous occu-pation of its progenitor – was the first mani-festation of Agnelli's declared intention to reach much wider markets than before and, by so doing, to satisfy a public need. Although the new factory was finished and the machinery of mass production installed in time for the launch of the

A 1922 two-seat 501, in this case with a Turpin body.

new car, industrial troubles inspired by Communist factions delayed the start of manufacture by some months. However, cars did eventually start to leave the line later in the year and these were snapped up by the motoring public.

There was nothing remarkable about the 501, which was a conventional front-engined, rear-wheel-drive machine. Its 1460cc, side-valve, four-cylinder power unit produced a somewhat lowly 23 bhp at 2600 rpm, which reached the rear wheels via a multi-plate clutch, a four-speed gearbox and a spiral-bevel final drive unit. The engine was, in fact, a direct development of that used in Cavalli's slightly earlier type 70, although its dimensions were different. Suspension was fairly unsophisticated, although common for the period, with semi-elliptic leaf springs front and rear. Braking effort was concentrated on the rear wheels, for both foot and hand brakes, something which was unusual on a car of this size.

The car was generally well received by the Press, particularly for its smooth ride and engine and its remarkably baulk-free gearbox, not to mention the luxurious appointment of the saloon bodies. For instance, *The Autocar*, in a road test, said: 'From the very start the car immediately suggests to the driver that sense of goodness – it is hard to describe it otherwise – which characterises any high-class automobile.'

However, the 501 certainly had its faults: it was heavy – the tourer weighed nearly 1 tonne; the engine was over-cooled, with its quite modern pump-and-fan system; gearing was too low, ratios being 25, 14, 10 and 5:1 for first to fourth gears respectively; with a combination of the low power output, the low gearing and the high overall weight, the top speed of the car was correspondingly low, at 85 km/h (53 mph) in open form and 74 km/h (46 mph) with the saloon body. Perhaps the most serious fault of all lay in the efficiency of the brakes; rear brakes alone cannot be expected to be more than adequate, but those on the 501 were very poor. However, they were markedly improved in 1922, when new linings were fitted, so perhaps the fault lay with the suppliers rather than with Fiat.

Even in this 1921 open two-seat form, the Fiat 501 could manage only 85 km/h (53 mph).

This 1925 saloon is equipped with pneumatic tyres, which were offered as an option from 1924 on.

Despite these faults and the fact that the 501 was not cheap, orders flooded in and a large export potential was realised. Known as the 10CV in France, the Eleven in England – and even being called the Sixteen in Rome – the little Fiat was responsible for 8000 out of a total of 14 000 Fiat export sales in 1923. The standard Fiat coachwork was somewhat crude, not to mention ugly, and this made it rather unpopular. Fortunately, several British coachbuilders offered bodies for the 501 and it was even found that bodies from the moribund Harper & Bean concern would fit the chassis with only minor modification.

Few changes were made throughout the life of the 501. Four-wheel brakes finally became an optional extra in 1924, replacing the still poor wire-operated items which had been inherited from the type 70, and pneumatic tyres were added to the list at the same time. Ignition had always been by high-tension magneto, but this had never prevented Cavalli from specifying full electric lighting in his plans for the car, so there

was no need for any modification in this area.

In 1923, a 501C (C for Coloniale) version of the car was introduced, with a reduction in weight of 100 kg (220 lb) and widened front and rear track, but the most important development had already taken place, in 1921, when the 501S sports car first saw the light of day. Like its big brother, the S could be obtained with several different body styles, although the standard apparel had a duck tail and was not unlike the Alvis 12/50. The engine's compression ratio was raised from 4.3:1 to 5.5:1 and this increased the power output to 26 bhp at 3000 rpm and gave a maximum speed in the region of 97 km/h (60 mph). Even more power could be squeezed out of the engine by the use of special pistons and a higher-compression head and a higher final-drive ratio of 4.6:1 was available to make this power more useful.

The Silvani tuning company, owned by a noted driver of that name, developed an overhead-valve cylinder head for the car, which was offered in 1924 and raised the power output to 35 bhp. Top speed with this head on the standard car was about 125 km/h (78 mph), although 143 km/h (89 mph) was claimed for a 501S thus equipped.

Many competition successes were gained by the S in varied forms of motor sport, although the 501SS, which was much more a pure racing car, was actually a type 802 and, apart from the radiator grille and certain dimensions, shared little with the 501, even having a double-overhead-camshaft engine.

A 1922 Fiat 501S, with body by Franchetti. This sports version was only slightly faster than standard.

When the model was finally replaced by the more sophisticated 503, in February 1926, nearly 80000 examples had been sold around the world and many thousands, particularly the taxi and light-van versions, were still running daily decades later. Perhaps the key to the 501's success lay not in what it could achieve but in the manner in which it achieved it: it was easy to drive, it ran smoothly and, most importantly, it did so for hundreds of thousands of miles.

PEUGEOT QUADRILETTE

In the years around World War 1, Peugeot of France had one of the more successful small-car designs, their second car to be known as the Bébé. This was particularly noteworthy because it was designed by Ettore Bugatti, but he decided that it was not right for his company and he sold the project to Peugeot, who then continued development and put the car into production. The beauty of this machine was that it was a real motor car, rather than a couple of bicycles joined together and powered. It is said, indeed, that had it not been for the wasted 4 years of World War 1 the Bébé would have been one of the world's best-sellers.

When the War ended in 1918, Peugeot realised that there would be an enormous market for a cheap but really practical small car – one which would provide transport for millions of people who could not afford existing vehicles but who really did need to move around. Whereas the Bébé had been a scaled-down version of a big car, the new machine would be basic, with just enough room for two people and just enough power to avoid excessive embarrassment on steep hills. Nevertheless, the Peugeot was to be more than a cyclecar: it would be basic rather than crude.

The new car was first shown to an eager public in 1919 at the first Paris Salon to be held after the War. It was hailed as a sensation, because although it would attract only the same annual road tax as the more common, extremely primitive cyclecars of the day, it was patently far more sophisticated than any other cyclecar.

Although the bodywork looked conventional from most points of view, with a front bonnet and side doors, it was set apart from the average machine by the fact that its two seats were mounted one behind the other in a body which was only 114 cm (45 in) or so wide. The driver's door was fitted to the left-hand side of the open tourer body, while the passenger entered by the right-hand side. The chassis was equally unconventional, in that it took the form of a pressed-steel punt, with box-section side members for extra stiffness.

In 1922, the Quadrilette was offered with staggered, side-by-side seating in a stretched body.

Unlike other cyclecars, La Quadrilette, as the new baby car was known, was equipped with a common four-cylinder engine, admittedly of only small capacity, at 628cc. This unit, which was water-cooled, gave out only 9½ bhp, but the car was so light that this was just about enough; it had a fixed cylinder head and side-mounted valves and was probably not very efficient, but it was much better than the more usual single- or twin-cylinder cyclecar engine, and had another advanced feature in the form of two ball main bearings.

A multi-plate clutch was mounted in unit with the engine and ran in an oil bath; this was usual enough for the period, but the Quadrilette departed from standard practice again with its gearbox, which was mounted in unit with the rear axle, thus pre-empting several more modern designs, such as the Alfa Romeo Alfettas, the Ferrari Daytona and the Porsche 924. This

The original Quadrilette of 1921, with its tandem seating and offset doors.

three-speed box, which had no synchromesh, was driven by a propeller shaft running in a torque tube – also serving to give positive location to the axle. Final drive was by worm gear and pinion and the rear track was narrow enough, at only 75 cm (29½ in), to make a differential unnecessary.

Suspension at the front was by a beam axle hung on a transverse leaf spring and located by radius arms. At the rear, quarter-elliptic leaf springs bore the weight. No dampers were fitted at all. Brakes were very primitive, although they managed the weight of the car; they were fitted only to the two rear wheels, but the right was operated by a hand lever and the left by a foot pedal.

The engine's electrical system was somewhat basic, there being no starter and no dynamo, and acetylene lights had to be relied on at night. Wheels were spoked and the spokes were of the tangential variety, as opposed to the radial type, which were markedly inferior with regard to torque capacity, of the Bébé.

Although the Quadrilette was announced in 1919, it took until 1921 for it to go on sale, by which time the public was very eager to own it, the post-war boom turning into a slump. Peugeot claimed fantastic capabilities for the new baby, only some of which were possibly a little coloured. It was certainly true that the Quadrilette could manage over 4.7 l/100 km (60 mpg)

and that it did not use excessive amounts of oil, but the company forgot to mention that, despite its miniscule weight, the little machine had almost non-existent performance.

Handling was certainly good and the car was very nimble, a feature which was enhanced by the narrowness of the body. Brakes took some getting used to but they seemed to work well enough. Most importantly, because of the low price, the Quadrilette represented motorised transport of a practical nature for everyman, as had been envisaged by Peugeot. Indeed, the company boasted the claim that the Quadrilette could complete a journey at less than one-third the cost of the equivalent third-class rail ticket.

Still with the narrow track, this 1922 saloon featured very unusual bodywork.

The company soon realised that the performance was not enough even for this type of car and the capacity of the engine was raised slightly to 667cc. Almost immediately, too, the bodywork began to be stretched: in 1922, the Quadrilette was offered with almost side-by-side seating, in which the passenger sat alongside and slightly behind the driver. Over the next few years, the bodywork became steadily larger until, by 1929, five-seat coachwork was fitted.

A more conventional chassis was incorporated in 1923, while 2 years later the engine again grew, this time to 719cc, although the last of the line, built in 1929, were reduced to 694cc, for some strange reason. A development of the Quadrilette, known as the 5CV, was announced in 1924; this had a similar mechanical layout, but was a more conventional car and by 1929 this had been endowed with a 950cc engine (with a detachable cylinder head) and front brakes.

The Peugeot Quadrilette did not sell in millions, but it did bring motoring to a new range of people and as a result had a long and prosperous life. It was particularly significant in that it represented a large step away from the image that baby cars had of being as crude as possible. Although the Austin Seven undoubtedly took this a stage further, the little Peugeot was responsible for making the public aware of the cyclecar's pitfalls. Had the Quadrilette not come from the house of Peugeot or a similar such distinguished company, then it might not have attained such a distinguished position in motoring's hall of fame; this would not have detracted from its importance, however.

Apparent conventionality in this 1922 two-seat Quadrilette, with its pretty bodywork.

AUSTIN SEVEN

During World War 1, Herbert Austin's Longbridge factory in Great Britain was turned over to the production of all types of munitions, from shells to aircraft and from gun carriages to armoured cars; indeed, it was for this work that Austin was knighted. At the end of the War there was a motoring boom and Austin decided to concentrate on manufacturing one model only in order to satisfy this demand. This policy may have been a good one, but the car, the Austin Twenty, was certainly wrong, for the price at which it was announced proved to be totally unrealistic and had to be increased by about 40 per cent almost immediately. This, coupled with the fact that the boom was very short-lived, caused a disastrous drop in sales – so much so that a Receiver had to be called in to try to sort out the mess.

The Austin Heavy Twelve, which followed shortly, soon set the company back on the right road, but this was little more than a small version of the Twenty and was by no means a trend-setter. By this time, however, Austin had decided that a whole new market lay in a baby car more sophisticated than the nasty cyclecars but cheap enough for people who hitherto found proper motoring too expensive for them. He suggested this to his colleagues at the works, but they laughed at him, wanting instead to carry on with the traditional style of Austin. Sir Herbert's answer was to convert the billiard room at his home into a drawing office and, with the help of one young draughtsman, set about designing his new baby.

Austin's brief to himself was to plan a car which covered no more ground area than an average motor cycle combination, but which offered seating for four people. He achieved these aims with his new Austin Seven, although there was certainly no 'extra' space in it. He originally planned to use a horizontally opposed twin-cylinder engine, but the prototype ran so roughly that he abandoned this unit in favour of an in-line four of 696cc. Even this was found to lack power, so it was enlarged for the production cars to 747cc, in which form this crude but rugged side-valve, two-bearing unit produced about 10 bhp – hardly enough to cope with the weight of the body plus four passengers.

Not surprisingly, the construction of the whole car was simple, a crude A-shaped chassis forming its basis. Suspension was by a transverse leaf spring at the front and quarter-elliptic springs at the rear, the live rear axle being connected to a centre propeller shaft bearing by a torque tube. A three-speed crash gearbox was standard on the first cars and although the Seven could claim the rare luxury of four-wheel brakes, the foot brake operated the rear wheels and the hand brake the front wheels. Initially, only a two-door tourer body was offered, but saloon variants soon followed and it was not long before bodywork of just about any type could be specified.

When it was announced in mid-1922 by a delighted Sir Herbert, the Austin Seven was greeted with a considerable amount of derision by the Press, who looked on it as a toy rather than a serious addition to the motoring market place. The already notable aviator, E. C. Gordon England, reckoned that he could remedy this situation and he challenged Austin to make him a racing version before his leg, broken in a flying accident, healed. Sir Herbert, who was totally opposed to the idea of a racing version, could not resist the challenge, built the car even more quickly than expected and was rewarded by Gordon England taking several records at Brooklands. The scheme paid off and the Seven immediately won the public over, killing off the primitive cyclecars at a stroke.

By the end of 1922, the initial price had been reduced and the orders were flooding in. Although the standard model was capable of only about 72 km/h (45 mph), sporting development continued apace, with Gordon England and Austin's son-in-law, Arthur Waite, as guiding lights. Gordon England sold his own lightweight sports and saloon bodies for the baby car, while Waite developed a Cozette-supercharged version of the engine with which, in 1931, the Seven became the first 750cc car to exceed 161 km/h (100 mph).

On the roadgoing front, the Seven story was one of continuous development, modifications being made to the chassis and to the engine to

One of the most famous coachbuilt Austin Seven bodies of all, the 1927 Swallow, from the pen of William Lyons.

The epitome of the Austin Seven, the spartan but effective Chummy version of 1923, with open top and two seats.

By 1936, body styling had altered beyond recognition, but beneath the skin lay the same basic Seven.

Complete with period luggage, this is a coachbuilt
Austin Seven saloon of 1928 vintage.

This 1936 Opal convertible was one of the many
body styles available in the Austin Seven range.

One of the sporting versions of the Seven, the extremely pretty Nippy of 1935.

improve the breed. Such luxuries as an electric starter, coil ignition and a four-speed gearbox were added in 1924, 1927 and 1933, respectively, and the brakes were at last coupled in 1930. Coachwork was provided by many concerns apart from Austin, notably Mulliner and Swallow (William Lyons's sidecar-building company, which by 1945 had become Jaguar), so there was a body for every occasion, ranging from the stark sportster to the elegant Top Hat saloon, so named because it was tall enough for a gentleman to enter without first removing his top hat.

In the early 1930s Austin commissioned Murray Jamieson to design a new version of the engine to power his racing cars and the result was a delightful twin-overhead-camshaft unit which, after some development, became one of the best engines in its class, powering specially built single-seater cars to countless victories. The standard unit could not match the 120 bhp of the twin-cam, but it did undergo some development itself during the 1930s, gaining a third main bearing, pressure lubrication and, finally, a 17 bhp power output. Even synchromesh was offered in 1933, so that, but for the original, vaguely located, bumpy and damperless suspension, which persisted to the end, the Seven might have had even wider appeal.

From the beginning to the end, which finally came in 1939, sales of this amazing little car were rapid. Surprisingly, the price of the basic model, although it fluctuated over the years, never rose much above the original and a cheaper grey-only version was briefly produced in the mid-1930s. The Seven was so successful that several foreign companies built the car under licence for their own markets. Notable examples were Dixi – later BMW – in Germany, Rosengart in France, Bantam in the USA and Datsun in Japan, although the Datsun seems to have been an illegal copy.

Towards the end of its life, the Seven, in common with the rest of the Austin range, underwent some styling changes, which included more aerodynamic bodywork and a new radiator shell, neither of which impressed Sir Herbert – by now Lord – Austin, who was opposed to following fashion. However, time finally caught up with his little wonder car and, in 1939, after over a quarter of a million examples had left the production line, the Seven was replaced by a new 900cc, 8 hp car. This was hardly the conclusion of the story, though, because the Seven formed the basis for vast numbers of little specials for many years thereafter and Reliant continued to manufacture their own version of the Austin engine until 1962.

CLYNO 10.8 HP

Like many of the early car manufacturers, Clyno started life in the motor cycle business. Two young cousins, Frank and Alwyn Smith, designed a form of variable-ratio pulley arrangement during the 1890s, for use on otherwise single-geared motor cycles, in order to help them in climbing hills. It was from this pulley, the variation in diameter of which was based on an inclined-plane system, that the Clyno name came.

It was not long before the cousins had moved into the assembly of complete motor cycles, using proprietary parts, and this they continued to do with some success until World War 1. In 1913, Frank Smith had shown an interest in cars by taking on a designer to plan such a machine, but the War intervened and his plans came to nothing, the company concentrating on the manufacture of military motor cycles and combinations, not to mention the assembly of various aero engines.

After the War, the design was updated and a prototype built, but the motoring sales boom which had followed the Armistice suddenly collapsed and the company could not sustain itself through the resultant hard times, backing having been withdrawn.

Nevertheless, a new concern rose out of the ashes in July 1922, when Frank Smith, as Managing Director, and his father William, as Chairman, formed the Clyno Engineering Company (1922) Ltd. Almost immediately, the original design was revived, although it was much modified by George Starley, who had been brought in as designer from Triumph Motor Cycles, and A. G. Booth, who was responsible for the detail work despite not being able to drive.

The Press was abuzz with rumours about the new car and most of these proved true. When the new machine, the 10.8 hp model, was announced late in 1922, it was certainly impressive, being well finished and the four-seater version being offered for a price which, in the pre-price-cutting days, was extremely reasonable. The 10.8 was obviously aimed to compete with Morris, both in price and in specification, and it seemed that there was no reason why it should not succeed.

The engine was actually manufactured by Coventry Climax and not Clyno and it was a straightforward side-valve four, with a capacity of 1368cc and a power output of around 20 bhp. The crankshaft was mounted in two ball races, which seemed adequate enough at the time, and the unit was water-cooled. A cone clutch was conventionally mounted in unit with the engine, but the gearbox arrangement was extremely novel. The box itself was straightforward enough, being a three-speed, unsynchronised unit, but it was connected to the clutch by a short, universally-jointed propeller shaft and was mounted at the forward end of a torque tube. The tube was joined to the rear axle casing in the conventional way, housing the rear propeller shaft, but the whole assembly pivoted about the gearbox mounting and this was most unusual. A spiral-bevel final-drive unit took the power to the rear wheels, but no differential was fitted, something which must have placed a great deal of strain on the half shafts.

Suspension was by quarter-elliptic leaves at front and rear, but these were not aided by any form of dampers. Steering was by worm-and-nut and the brakes, which operated only on the rear wheels, were somewhat crude, one side being worked by a foot pedal and the other by the hand lever. The chassis itself was conventional, with a ladder-type arrangement in a mixture of channel-section and tubular steel.

Various body styles were offered by Clyno, ranging from tourers to saloons, and all were reasonably priced. The concept was certainly a winning one, for not only did the Press acclaim the 10.8 but the agents clamoured to get their hands on as many examples as they could and the public in turn loved the car. Orders poured in to such an extent that output could not meet demand. By August 1923, motor cycle production, which the new concern had continued, had ceased and the factory was reorganised to meet the orders for the 10.8; as a happy result of increasing production, it was possible to reduce the price of the four-seat saloon, which brought even more entries for the already bulging order book.

During the first year of production, only 623

Overleaf. A 1927 Clyno 10.8 hp Royal tourer, with bodywork by H.J.Mulliner. Despite its high price, this was a best-selling model.

This 1923 two-seat version of the Clyno was one of the earliest examples.

cars were built, but this was almost exclusively due to the initial hiatus in the works. In that period the directors and staff were making a conscious effort to campaign the car in competition as much as possible, a plan which paid off handsomely, with a string of victories in trials and in circuit events – all a healthy sign for sales.

The bombshell was dropped at the London Motor Show in October 1923, when Morris announced that they were cutting their prices. Clyno felt that they had to follow suit, so they matched Morris's price exactly, and this marked the beginning of a long and bitter price war which Clyno could only lose in the end, not having Morris's relatively vast resources. It was not that sales did not boom – things could not have looked healthier from that point of view – it was more that profit margins had been pared to the bone and it was therefore essential to make more cars in

order to make ends meet. One good thing came out of the war, and that was Clyno's slogan, which read: 'A price level as low as any car of like rating in the world – and a value vastly higher.' This was probably true, since an improved specification went along with the reduced price: a differential became an optional extra (and was made a standard fitting not long after) and bodywork and lighting standards were raised.

April of 1924 saw the first really important development for the 10.8, when the Colonial model was announced. This was produced with export in mind and was thus equipped with wider track, greater ground clearance and a larger radiator; the Colonial was a great success abroad, being suitable for fairly harsh treatment on rough roads and in hot climates, and sales figures for this period were generally extremely healthy. Two months after the Colonial came a sporting version of the 10.8, which was a tuned two-seater with very special bodywork and an outside exhaust pipe. Due to the demand for the standard models and the consequent lack of production capacity, only twenty-five examples of the Sport were made, but it did carry the distinction of being the first Clyno to be fitted with four-wheel brakes as standard.

At the London Motor Show of 1924, these brakes became an option on the normal models and balloon tyres became standard fittings, along with a prestigious right-hand gearchange. Several new versions were announced, principally a new Weymann-bodied saloon and the Royal Clynos, the latter of which came in a number of saloon and tourer forms, all with coachbuilt bodies by Mulliner. Prices were reduced again by both Morris and Clyno, but sales seemed to be ever on the up, the figure for 1925 being 4849.

During 1925, the faithful roller bearings on the crankshaft were discarded in favour of more conventional plain shells and the 1925 Motor Show saw the introduction of a new model, with Clyno's own 11.9 hp engine. 1926 saw the sales of the 10.8 reach a peak, with 350 cars a week leaving the factory, but then orders began to tail off and new models simply could not recover them.

The company probably became too ambitious at this stage, because the Smiths built a new, massive factory at Wolverhampton, for which they could not pay and then production of the 10.8 – from the old plant – began to dwindle. Improvements were made to the car during 1926, among them being the adoption of four-wheel brakes as standard, together with semi-elliptic front springs. Although price-cutting was still going on at this stage, it should have been obvious that it was unnecessary, since the more expensive Royals were selling far better than their much cheaper stablemates.

Total production for 1927 was 7350 and the updated model of the following year, which was enlarged and had a different radiator design, was no longer popular – indeed, the *aficionados* considered it a retrograde step. Sadly, although the price war ended in 1928, it was really too late to save this fine little car and its manufacturer and, while the 10.8 struggled on into 1929, Clyno finally had to close their doors, with an impressive total of 11 149 of the 10.8 hp under their belt.

RILEY NINE

Riley was an old established family concern by the time work started on a new breed in the mid-1920s. William Riley had founded a cycle-building company in 1890 and he and his four sons had gradually moved into car manufacture. However, these individuals did not always see eye to eye, so there existed several disparate yet complementary branches of the Riley 'empire'.

World War 1 saw the company concentrating on supplying munitions for the troops from its various factories, and in this way the family business survived well. The first new model of Riley car after the War had a side-valve engine. It sold quite well and functioned effectively; the most noteworthy version of this machine was the pretty little sportster, now very famous as the Redwinger.

In the early part of the 1920s, Percy Riley, who was the real family engine genius, had been devoting most of his time to projects outside the motor industry, stationary engines and so on, but his fingers soon began to itch and he sat down to plan a new car engine, with the help of his brother Stanley. The results of his efforts were astonishingly modern – so much so that one of the motors which he created then would not, in concept at least, seem especially old-fashioned today.

The most remarkable feature of this 1087cc, four-cylinder unit was its valve arrangement: overhead valves were inclined in hemispherical combustion chambers and operated by two camshafts mounted high up, one each side of the block, via short pushrods and rockers. This arrangement gave the overhead camshafts the advantage of low valve gear mass and ideal valve position with the simplicity of tappet adjustment of the pushrod engine. The camshafts were gear-driven from the crankshaft, by way of an idler gear, and these gears also drove the magneto and a novel double-plunger oil pump.

The crankshaft itself had only two main bearings, but the whole assembly was extremely sturdy and both the mains and the big ends were pressure-fed with oil. Not only was the new power unit a triumph of design, it was very carefully made and this soon helped it to gain a

A late edition of the Riley Monaco, built in 1933 with Weymann construction.

This 1928 Monaco saloon is similar in appearance to its later Weymann equivalent, yet it has a fabric body.

reputation for reliability. Not only did it seem to be a modern engine; its worth was well proved by the fact that a close derivative of it remained the mainstay of Riley power output until 1957, by which time the company had seen two changes of ownership.

The new power plant was first shown in mid-1926, when it was fitted to an extremely stylish fabric saloon, known as the 9 hp Monaco, and a design from the inspired pen of Stanley Riley. This car, with its low lines (made possible by the inclusion of deep footwells for the rear-seat passengers) and its unusual built-in luggage boot, was an immediate success, so much so that the company was not fully prepared to meet demand. The price must have had something to do with this, for it was very reasonable for the luxurious specification offered. More incredible was the fact that Riley managed to hold the Monaco at the same price from its launch to its

eventual withdrawal in 1938; the explanation was that models were priced according to demand — and the Monaco was always in great demand.

The chassis of the new car was a straight-forward perimeter frame, with channel-section side members and channel and tubular cross members. The engine was mounted at the front, in the conventional manner, and a single-dry-plate clutch took the drive to a four-speed gearbox mounted in unit with the engine. A torque tube joined the gearbox to a live rear axle; a propeller shaft and spiral-bevel final-drive unit drove the half shafts.

Semi-elliptic springs were fitted all round, with friction dampers at the front and hydraulics

A Riley Imp two-seat sports car of 1935. Introduced in 1934, this was based on a shortened Nine chassis.

at the rear. Steering relied on a worm-drive box and cable-operated mechanical brakes were standard equipment on all four wheels.

The Nine performed extremely well: its engine produced a modest 27 bhp or so, but this was sufficient to propel the 914 kg (18 cwt) Monaco at over 97 km/h (60 mph), which was a very respectable speed for the day. A constant-mesh silent third gear was fitted and this was intended for use at average cruising speeds. Riley were delighted with the success of their new machine, which they had christened The Wonder Car, and they stopped production of the earlier models in 1928, in order to satisfy demand for the Nine.

It was in 1927 that Parry Thomas, the record-breaking ace, decided that the Nine had a great deal of competition potential. He began work on a racing version of the car, but unfortunately he was killed while this was still at an early stage. His

assistant, Reid Railton, continued with the plans with the result that the latter part of the year saw the Brooklands Nine, with a 50 bhp engine, 145 km/h (90 mph) top speed and a special body on a shortened chassis. The Brooklands car was immensely successful, winning handsomely on its first outing and taking many victories thereafter.

Mid-1929 saw the new Plus model of the Nine, with a stiffer chassis, better springs, stronger wheels and larger brakes, which were adjustable from the driver's seat. Brightwork was now of stainless steel and chassis lubrication could be controlled from a single point. A twin-carburettor version of the engine could be

The Lincock fixed-head two-seat coupé was one of several sporting Riley Nines. This example was made in 1933.

A 1936 Nine Lynx, a four-door open tourer.

specified, to boost the power output to 37 bhp and the top speed to around 112 km/h (70 mph).

Body styles began to proliferate in 1930, when the Monaco went over to Weymann construction; there was also an open tourer and a half-panelled saloon known as the Biarritz. In the following year, a dropped chassis was introduced and this had the effect of reducing the height of the cars, while at the same time dispensing with the need for the footwells in the Monaco. Body construction was further improved and two new models were added to the range – a sports two-seater called the Gamecock and a sturdy four-seater tourer for army use. The Nine series was now known as the Plus Ultra.

Body styling of the Monaco was altered considerably in 1932, when the windscreen acquired a greater angle and the rear passengers greater headroom. More new additions to the range appeared, among them a novel low saloon called the Falcon. This had Riley-patented 'roofdoors' built into the roof, so that they lifted up when the doors were opened, thus facilitating access to the car. One of the other 1932 models was known as the Trinity; this could be converted quickly from a two-seater to a four-seater and could be used in open or closed form.

Unfortunately, however, despite the originality of its design, the Trinity never sold very well.

The most important development of 1933 was the introduction of the Imp, a short-chassised sportster Nine, with a very pretty two-seat body. This did not actually reach production until early in the following year, but it, and its highly tuned sister, the Ulster Imp, were highly popular. Also for 1933, a Wilson pre-selector gearbox became an option, but this was dropped in 1935, in which year the chassis was strengthened again.

The dear old Monaco saloon finally gave way to a new, cheaper Merlin in 1935. However, this all-steel machine did not appeal to the fans and a new Monaco, also with a steel body, was announced for the London Motor Show of the following year.

By this time, a 1.5-litre equivalent of the engine had been announced and Riley were slowly getting deeper into financial trouble. Sales of the Nine range began to tail off in the face of in-house rivalry and the series was finally withdrawn at the end of 1938. The last of the run had been a new all-steel saloon called the Victor, whose launch had coincided with a take-over by the Nuffield Group; but a shadow of the Nine's former glory, it simply postponed the inevitable.

FORD MODEL A

The Model T Ford was completely Henry Ford's creation and it was such a massive success that the old man firmly believed that it would go on fulfilling the needs – and the wishes – of the motoring public into the unforeseeable future. Up to a point he was right: for 15 years or so there were no signs that the public wanted anything better. However, the main reason for this had to be the cheapness of the T, for it was crude in the extreme and offered nothing by way of luxury appointments.

By the early 1920s, Henry had made his son, Edsel, President of the company, although he still controlled its running from behind the scenes. It was Edsel Ford who first realised that the Model T's life was going to be of limited extent, with better quality cars coming from the opposition, such as Chevrolet (who were soon vying with Ford for the position of best-selling car manufacturer). He reasoned that a new mass-market vehicle would soon be needed – one which offered a more practical package than did the Model T but at the same sort of price; unfortunately, his father did not agree with this idea and devoted his time to a completely new type of engine which he thought should power the next generation of Fords when it eventually arrived.

Henry's new pet was an eight-cylinder unit with an 'X' configuration (as in two V4 engines joined by a common crankshaft). Several prototypes of this power unit were built, in both air-cooled and water-cooled form, between 1922 and the project's final abandonment in 1926; the concept was apparently quite a good one, the engines ran smoothly and powerfully (with steel instead of cast iron or aluminium pistons), but the cylinder layout did not lend itself conveniently to mounting in a car. The unit had to be mounted high up in the chassis, so that lower cylinders had clearance beneath them and even then, with an impossibly high drive line, mud and road dirt caused all sorts of troubles and the lower banks suffered from oil fouling. Henry Ford was quite convinced that the new Ford car could wait until he had solved all his new engine's

The most popular version of Ford's Model A was the Tudor two-door, four-seat sedan; this is a 1929 example.

problems, but Edsel, and several other top staff men, knew better; they were also sure that the X8 would be too complex for the Model T's replacement.

In the meantime, Edsel had been working on a new six-cylinder power unit, largely because other manufacturers were producing such engines with great success. However, Henry had lost all faith in such a configuration after the failure of his much earlier Model K and, despite the new motor showing considerable promise, refused to allow it to be used.

It was not until the end of 1926 that Henry Ford finally accepted that a new Ford would soon be needed and by then it was very nearly too late to avoid losing a great deal of money. Edsel Ford and his team came up with a much improved machine compared with the T; they designed a car that was more stylish than the T, while at the same time offering more space, more strength

A handsome two-seat cabriolet Model A of 1929, equipped with extraordinary Woodlite headlamps.

and generally more practicality. At every stage, there was a battle with the old man over the proposed specification. Every item had to be approved by him and this approval, when it was forthcoming, was only grudgingly given; it was not that he necessarily thought each design was bad, it was more that he was piqued because this was not 'his' baby in the same way as the T had been.

Regardless of delays caused by problems and changes of mind, the first of the new breed was designed and built by 20 October 1927 and actually went into production, albeit at only twenty a day, on 1 November. However, the T had been withdrawn, at a stroke, in June, so the company was in great danger of losing a massive

Four doors and four seats on this Weymann-bodied English Model A of 1930.

number of sales. Fortunately, word of the new car had deliberately been spread far and wide and the potential customers were so eager to see this new marvel that they were prepared to wait as long as it took. In fact they were even eager to place orders, ½ million of them, without a sight of the vehicle.

Although production began in a small way in November, announcement of the car to the public did not take place until 2 December. Public anticipation of this moment was staggering: people queued in the cold and wet of winter at dealers' showrooms all over America to catch a fleeting glimpse of the new masterpiece. The newspapers the next day were full of reports of hundreds of thousands of people packing the streets in the sort of sensational reception normally reserved for heroes of the hour or for the end of a war. Even then only 500 examples had been built, so there were many showrooms

which had only brochures and pictures to offer – still considered better than nothing by the populace. Moreover, the supply position was hopeless: unless production could be speeded up soon, and by a massive amount, it would take years to complete existing orders. Demand was so great that it was not long before Henry instructed that no further orders be taken until May 1928.

The specification of the new car was certainly better than that of its predecessor and it put the Model A, as it was known, into a new generation. Indeed, Ford claimed that he had reverted to the letter A (which he had used previously) to signify the beginning of a new age for Ford. Although he had not immediately given the Model A his full

A dickey seat was a useful extra on a two-seat soft-top model such as this 1931 example.

support, he was quick to acknowledge its worth and to compliment his son.

The 3.4-litre, four-cylinder engine was slightly bigger than that of the Model T, but it bore many resemblances. It retained its side valves and its three-bearing crankshaft, but the crank was stronger and aluminium pistons were used for the first time in a Ford. In its original form, the engine produced only 22 bhp, so an eminent engineer, Harold Hicks, was employed on condition that he would extract 40 bhp from the unit within 1 month. He changed the exhaust manifold, enlarged the valves and talked Ford into fitting a Zenith carburettor, as opposed to the inadequate unit from Ford's friend Holley,

and had the motor turning out the required 40 bhp in only 3 weeks.

A multi-plate dry clutch joined the front engine to a new gearbox, of the sliding-pinion type, with three forward speeds and reverse. A new transmission system had been essential for the Model A, that of its forebear being somewhat primitive. Henry Ford had wanted to use the same basic epicyclic arrangement, but to make gear changes automatic, and he was told that the necessary technicalities could not be designed quickly enough, so the more standard gearbox was used (needless to say, Ford had perceived what was later to become the normal arrangement for automatic transmission, although he had not come to terms with the necessary torque converter).

A torque tube linked gearbox and rear axle, the axle containing a spiral-bevel final-drive unit and a differential. The rear axle was also of the 'live' type, suspended on a somewhat crude transverse leaf spring. The front beam axle was also located in this way and this rather imprecise system, which did not do a great deal for handling, remained a Ford trademark for many years to come. At least the Model A was blessed with modern hydraulic dampers all round.

Steering was by worm-and-sector box, while four-wheel, mechanically operated brakes were fitted and operated by a foot pedal. The hand brake operated on the rear brakes, in the modern style.

There were five different body styles on the original car, which had a straightforward channel-section chassis. It is interesting to note that this was the first vehicle to be fitted with a laminated windscreen as standard. Harold Hicks was testing one of the prototypes when he was involved in an accident. He and his passenger were thrown through the windscreen and quite badly hurt (so much so in Hicks's case that he did no further work on the project), which led to the decision to fit the new glass.

Several changes to the specification were made early on in the A's life. Ford had a love of forgings, and tended to use them where a pressing was entirely adequate – and perhaps even better – and it took some time to talk him into allowing many of the complicated and expensive forgings on the A to be replaced. The early connecting rods were of either X or tubular section, but these were soon replaced by the stronger I-section items.

The price of the Model A was as staggering as its appearance and its specification: the Tudor cost only the same as the equivalent T had done. It subsequently turned out that the company had been losing on each Tudor sold, but this did achieve the desired effect of pushing up demand. Performance was better than that of the Model T: with more power and less weight, the A could

reach 112 km/h (70 mph) and had very sprightly acceleration to match.

The delay in getting production started at a sensible rate had been caused by the need to retool the plant at Rouge. However, when this was completed the cars began to come off the line much more quickly. By March 1928 the flow was up to 2000 cars per day and 3 months later this had quadrupled to 8000. By the end of that year, it was possible to begin making cars for the man in the street, all the advance orders having been satisfied. The original idea had been to have cars available at dealers for customers to walk in and buy and this was now feasible at last. Nearly 1 million cars were built in 1928 and by 1929 the Model A had regained for Ford the world lead that it had lost to Chevrolet in 1927.

The 1 millionth car actually left the line on 4 February 1929 and by July this figure had doubled. More models were added to the range until, in 1930, there were seventeen different options in the car range, plus commercials and a taxi variant.

Many changes were made to the Model A during its life, but most of them were either very minor or concerned the various body styles. The first major alteration came in November 1928, when the multi-disc clutch, which had given considerable trouble, was replaced by a single-disc one. In August of the following year, an electric windscreen wiper motor replaced the vacuum unit of the early cars. Larger balloon tyres were added in January 1930, and so the changes went on until the end of that year. At the end of 1931, Ford announced the revolutionary V8; as a safeguard, the Model A was continued in production until the end of April, when a new Model B (the V8 body with the four-cylinder engine) was introduced, but by then sales had fallen to a mere trickle, with only 905 cars manufactured.

It had been clear from the start that the Model A would not last as had done the T; the T was years ahead of its time, but the A was only just abreast of its time. The most remarkable fact is that, despite this, over 5 million examples were sold and owners were highly delighted with the machine. The reliability of the Model A can be judged by the number of cars still in everyday use thirty years later, when most of the competition

had long since gone to the scrapyard. The Model A may not have shown the innovation of its predecessor, but it provided just what the people wanted and did so at exactly the right price.

Another two-seat drop-head version of the A, again with a dickey seat for occasional passengers.

CHEVROLET INTERNATIONAL SIX

The name Billy Durant is legendary in the history of the American motor industry, for it crops up in the stories of so many famous companies; indeed, it is often the link between such concerns. One of this entrepreneurial character's early foundations was Buick and, through that, General Motors (GM); but, he expanded the company too quickly and too much and soon lost control of both Buick and General Motors. Undismayed, in 1910, he set racing driver Louis Chevrolet, who had worked for him at Buick, to work in a garage to design a new car. Chevrolet, assisted by an engineer, Etienne Planche, produced plans for two models, a four and a six, and Durant gave him the go ahead to build the six, which was to carry the Chevrolet name.

The Classic Six, as the car was known, was a success and the company, now known as the Chevrolet Motor Company of Michigan, quickly grew, until Durant was in a position to tempt General Motors' stockholders to exchange their shares for the more profitable Chevrolet ones. In this way, he gradually regained control of GM and in 1918 Chevrolet was formally incorporated into the conglomerate, the fifth and last division to be added.

At this time, Chevrolet had a tiny percentage of the market compared with Ford, but in 1915, Durant had taken his new concern into direct competition with Ford by announcing a rather crude new model, the 490, at Model T prices (490 represented the price in dollars). Although this car certainly boosted Chevrolet sales enormously, there was no way that the Model T could be beaten at its own game. It was not until 1927, when the Ford was withdrawn from production,

Little external change had taken place by 1931, but the International Six gained Chevrolet the top of the sales league.

that the 490's successor, the Superior, took the company into first place in the sales league, with sales of over 1 million.

In 1925, Chevrolet started to think in terms of a new straight-six engine, having produced a new one for General Motors' Pontiac division just before. At that time, the company had a slogan which read: 'Valves in head, ahead in value', so to comply with this, designer O. E. Hunt endowed the 3.2-litre unit with overhead valves operated by pushrods from a single side-mounted camshaft. Three crankshaft bearings were considered adequate, as was splash lubrication, but the most surprising feature of the motor was the incorporation of cast-iron pistons at a time when nearly all the competition had turned to light alloy. This, together with the use of a multitude of 0.6 cm ($\frac{1}{4}$ in) bolts to hold the unit in one piece, led to the engine being known alternatively as the 'Cast-iron Wonder' or the 'Stove-bolt Six'.

Fitted into a straightforward pressed-steel chassis, the engine was joined in the conventional way to a single-dry-plate clutch and a three-speed gearbox, in this instance without any synchromesh. A propeller shaft enclosed in a torque tube transmitted the drive to the live rear axle, which incorporated a spiral-bevel final-drive unit with a differential. Suspension was by semi-elliptic leaf springs at front and rear, with a forged front axle beam. Quite unusually for the period, hydraulic dampers were utilised, in this case the lever-arm type, which were used to give improved wheel location. The four-wheel drum brakes were mechanically operated and the car was steered by way of a worm-and-sector box.

A variety of body styles was offered, ranging from open tourers through cabriolets to four-door saloons, and the car was quite well equipped and finished for its price.

Announced in December 1928, the International Six, as it was officially known, was almost twice as powerful as the Superior it replaced and was every bit as good as Ford's new Model A, which was still relying on a four-cylinder engine. The 46 bhp which the Six

One of the first International Six Chevrolets to be built in 1929 was this four-door, seven-window sedan.

This four-door landaulette version of the International Six, with its artillery wheels, was made in 1929.

A four-door open-tourer Chevrolet, with coachwork by Fisher, manufactured in 1929.

produced endowed the car with sprightly performance and the suspension offered a far superior level of ride comfort to that of the Ford. The International was not averse to consuming its share of petrol, but this did not seem to worry the American public who, despite the Depression, were paying extremely little for their fuel.

The new car caught on immediately, appealing mainly because of its simplicity and its efficiency. One of the great advantages of this simplicity, which should not be confused with crudity, was that the International was very easy to repair – not that this was often necessary, as the machine was also very rugged.

Although Ford regained the sales lead in 1929 and 1930, with the new Model A, the International Six was an instant bestseller, with more than 1 million being produced during its first year. 1931 saw the top-of-the-league position going to Chevrolet again and it is a fact that, except for one or two years since that time, the company has always held that place.

The International was steadily revised and improved during its first few years, such items as

synchromesh gearboxes, rubber engine mountings and even a free-wheel being offered as standard fittings. Styling too was altered slightly, but the first major change came in 1933, when Harley Earl and a team of stylists brought in the Standard and Master models to replace the single International Six. The Master offered very much the earlier specification, but the Standard was a cheaper car, with a lower and lighter body and less luxurious appointments. The Standard was the cheapest Chevrolet ever made. Modernisation continued apace after that, the next major change being the introduction, in 1934, of independent front suspension, based on the 'knee-action' principle of France's André Dubonnet (of aperitif and motor racing fame). Although this suspension system was a standard item, it was curiously still possible to specify the old beam front axle on Chevrolets right up until 1940, when coils and wishbones were introduced.

Although the International Six was not strictly replaced, by the end of the 1930s the original concept had been modified so much that it could

One of the more fashionable body styles in 1929 was this two-seat cabriolet seen on Chevrolet's International Six.

no longer be seen as the same car. 1935 saw the end of the famous cabriolet versions and 1937 was the year in which the cars were extensively redesigned around a new standard wheelbase. At the same time, the famous old stove-bolt engine was completely reworked, with a four-bearing crankshaft and an increased capacity of 3.55 litres, and it was renamed the Blue Flame. Interestingly, the Blue Flame still retained the cast-iron pistons which had been antiquated back in 1928, and these, along with the splash lubrication of the bearings, were still features of very closely related engines in use as late as 1953.

The International Six, then, not only set Chevrolet on the road to success, it provided the basis for a whole series of cars, which formed the backbone of the Chevrolet range for many years.

FIAT 508 BALILLA

At the beginning of the 1930s, the Western world was in the depths of the Depression and the last few years had seen countless car manufacturing companies, many of them former household names, disappear for ever. Of the survivors, Fiat was probably best placed to endure these hard times, with a virtual monopoly of the Italian car market and almost a 'captive audience'. However, even this giant could not afford to be complacent, especially in view of the total failure of the type 514, which had been announced in 1929 and was the wrong car for the economic climate. Fiat management therefore decided that their next offering would be a 'European' model, which would attract vast export sales. As it turned out, the 508 Balilla, for this was the new machine's designation, exceeded these aims, for not only did it sell well abroad, but it was even manufactured under licence in France, Germany, Poland and Czechoslovakia.

The new family of light cars was the product of the fertile pen of Tranquillo Zerbi, who had been with the company since 1919 and had already designed both the legendary supercharged straight-eight for the 801 racer, a remarkably powerful two-stroke, double-six-cylinder racing engine which was only once raced – albeit successfully – and a double–V12 aero engine which powered its mount to a new air speed record. When ill-health forced Carlo Cavalli into retirement in 1928, Zerbi took over as Technical Director.

His 508 Balilla was announced at the Milan Motor Show of 1932, and appeared to be an updated version of the 509 concept. Contrary to popular belief, the name Balilla (=plucky little one) was not dedicated to a Fascist Youth group of the period, but was coined in memory of a young boy who was a hero of the revolt against the Austrians at the end of the eighteenth century. In its original form, the Balilla was equipped with a compact tourer body which helped to keep the overall weight of the car down and its performance up. The three-bearing, four-

The winning feature of Fiat's 508S was the car's pretty body, as admirably displayed on this 1935 example.

cylinder engine was simplicity itself, having side valves, but its beauty lay in the fact that its 995cc capacity was achieved by almost 'square' dimensions of 65 mm bore and of 75 mm stroke, something that was very rare at the time. This allowed high engine speeds to be maintained without damage so that, despite producing only 22 bhp, this power unit gave the little Balilla better performance than the sophisticated overhead-cam machinery of approximately the same capacity endowed upon the 509A.

A single-plate clutch transmitted drive to a three-speed gearbox mounted in unit with the engine. Somewhat surprisingly, synchromesh was not fitted to any of the gears and gear-changing was not helped by rather wide ratios of 5.2, 9.5 and 14.9:1 overall, in top, second and first respectively. An open propeller shaft joined the gearbox to the live rear axle, which had a spiral-bevel final drive with a ratio of 4.89:1.

An early 508 Balilla, in this case a two-door, four-seat saloon of 1932.

A beam axle was also utilised at the front and suspension was by semi-elliptic leaf springs all round, with hydraulic dampers available as an optional extra (strangely, friction dampers became the standard fitting on later cars, which today seems something of a retrograde step). Hydraulic brakes were fitted and were certainly a rarity in those days; a transmission handbrake took care of parking.

There were several other features of the Balilla which were advanced, particularly for a car of this class: a 12-volt electrical system was standard, as was a hand throttle – which was common to all Fiats until the mid 1960s; even a free-wheel was offered as an option. An alternative two-door saloon body was available on the

same separate cross-braced chassis, as was a military two-seater, with extra ground clearance and a special body, and a light van. The prices in Italy both for the tourer and the saloon were very reasonable.

A slightly tuned version of the engine was offered as an extra; this Spinto unit, as it was known, produced 28 bhp by virtue of an increased compression ratio. Indeed, although in standard form power output was modest, the almost unburstable nature of the engine made it eminently tuneable, the only mechanical limitation being a tendency for the crankshaft to snap at the then extremely high speed of 6300 rpm.

The Balilla was an immediate success, probably due to its impressive specification and its low price, but it sustained this success by living up to its promise. Contemporary road tests carried out by the top motoring magazines show that it was very popular with the Press, having lively

A rare example of a four-door Balilla, made in 1933, equipped with a three-speed gearbox.

performance and handling well. 1933 saw it begin to make its mark in competition, an overhead valve conversion and a four-speed gearbox helping some cars considerably, although much more standard examples also acquitted themselves well.

Late in the year, downdraught carburation became standard, but, more importantly, a four-door pillarless saloon was added to the range – still based on the same chassis – and this was joined by the first sporting version of the car, the 508S.

The 508S was considerably more expensive than any other version and produced only a little more power, at 30 bhp. Various other mechanical modifications were incorporated, the most important being friction dampers, but the 508S's real winning feature was its pretty open two-seat body; this helped the car to a maximum speed of nearly 112 km/h (70 mph), which compared well with the under 96 km/h (60 mph) top of the original tourer.

In 1934, the 'standard' cars were modified again. The wheelbase was lengthened to improve the four-door saloon, which still had the same basic body as before, and a four-speed gearbox, with synchromesh on the top two ratios, became standard on all the 508 models. In addition to this the power output of the standard engine was raised a little to cope with the extra weight of the new chassis. A variety of body styles was now appearing from the various styling houses or coachbuilders; there was even a cabriolet.

The 508S underwent considerable change in 1934, perhaps the most significant being the adoption of a 36 bhp pushrod engine which boosted performance considerably. Two different body styles were now listed; these were both open versions – the Sport, with flared wings and the Corsa-Coppa d'Oro, with a narrower body, cycle wings and no running boards; in addition, a fastback coupé was announced in the following year and was known as the Berlinetta Aerodynamica. The S was by no means a perfect car, but it was certainly successful – both in terms of sales and of competition victories. The Press dubbed it a 'fun car' and it seems to have been there that its appeal lay. It had a top speed of over 112 km/h (70 mph), it handled and stopped well and it was attractive; what is more, it dominated the 1100cc class in racing for two seasons, tuned by many amateurs and professionals alike. Amédée Gordini, 'The Sorcerer', probably

The Fiat 508C, which replaced the Balilla in 1937, was an all-new car despite its shared type number.

obtained more power than anyone else from the engine – over 50 bhp was eventually squeezed from it without resorting to supercharging.

For a brief period in 1936, the saloon was offered with some of the S parts, mainly the pushrod engine. This car was also successful in competition, but only about 1000 were sold. 1935 was probably the Balilla's best year, the factory turning cars out at a rate of 500 per week. Strangely, sales dropped drastically in 1936, however, and by the time this fine little machine was replaced by the all-new 508C in 1937 output was down to a trickle. In all, about 114000 Balillas were built, around 2000 of which were the S version. In 5 short years the car made a considerable impact on the motoring public.

FORD MODEL Y

Henry Ford's Model T is probably the most famous motor car ever built, only having been outsold by the Volkswagen 'Beetle' – and then at a time when the numbers of the car-buying public had grown many times over. The Model A, which finally replaced it in 1927, was also a great success, even if it did not achieve the distinction of the T. However, sales of the Model A in Great Britain, Ford of Britain having been established as a separate company, soon began to dwindle, probably because of the punitive system of road tax, whereby no matter how powerful the engine actually was, tax was collected according to a horsepower formula based on engine capacity. Ford even tried marketing a special sleeved-down version of the car, which would be cheaper to run in Britain, but this performed so badly that it was not at all popular.

In 1928, Henry Ford showed some drawings of a proposed new light car to Sir Percival Perry, Chairman of Ford of Britain, the idea being that this car would compete with the extremely successful Austin Seven. Perry was not impressed by the design, however, remaining firmly convinced that the small car did not show the way

to the stars; he reasoned that the Model T was so massive a winner that another model in that mould could only lead to even greater things. Undeterred by this rejection, Ford had fifteen competitive light cars from various European countries shipped to the USA so that he could evaluate their quality and their performance. This was in 1930, but, by the beginning of 1931, ever-falling sales figures had miraculously converted the sceptical Sir Percival Perry and he wrote to Henry Ford's son, Edsel, telling him: 'Everyone in this country is agreed that the only path out of the present intense industrial depression is one of economy, and as this reacts upon the motor industry it means that the tendency everywhere is to buy smaller and cheaper motor cars.'

Henry did not respond to this change of heart but, by October, Perry was desperate and he wrote to the great man pleading with him for a new light car to save Ford of Britain and its newly

The two-door Model Y saloon in its original form of 1932.

opened Dagenham factory. Sales of light cars had been on the increase, despite the generally appalling figures for larger vehicles, and this time Henry Ford started work immediately on the new machine. Development of the light car progressed like lightning, with even the boss turning his hand to a spanner in order to speed production of the prototypes. Indeed, it seems likely that the gestation period of the new car was shorter than that of any other before or since, as between October 1931 and February 1932 the vehicle was designed and developed and sixteen prototypes constructed, under the guidance not only of Henry himself but of his Chief Engineer, Laurence Sheldrick.

There was some argument between Ford and Perry over what the new model should be called; Ford wanted to coin the name Mercury, but Perry insisted that the Ford title be retained, as this would attract a number of buyers who might otherwise be deterred. On this occasion Sir Percival won the battle and the new baby car was unveiled at the Albert Hall Ford Exhibition of February 1932 as the Ford Model Y.

The car immediately caused something of a sensation, because, despite styling reminiscent of a much larger car, and accommodation to match, it was on offer, for the fully equipped four-door version, at a price which undercut both the Morris Minor and the Austin Seven. Widely acclaimed by dealers, Press and public alike, the Model Y went on general sale in Britain only a year after Perry's begging letter to Ford. It was the first Ford to have been designed especially for the British market and it was also the last (along with the V8) in which Henry Ford took a personal interest.

Technically the Model Y, which was rated as an 8 hp car, was somewhat staid. The 933cc engine was a water-cooled side-valve four, mounted at the front; this did feature the fairly modern refinement of a three-bearing crankshaft, which made it more sturdy and more reliable. The engine fed its power via a dry-plate clutch to a three-speed gearbox, itself fairly luxurious in

A 1934 Ford Model Y. This was the first car from Ford to be designed exclusively for the European market.

having synchromesh on second and top gears; in fact this was the first under 1000cc popular car to be so equipped, so the specification was not totally mundane. The power reached the rear wheels by way of a propeller shaft and a live rear axle, suspended, as was the front, on a transverse leaf spring.

Rod-operation for the drum brakes was retained from earlier models, as was the central accelerator pedal. However, wire wheels were offered as a standard fitting and the well finished body came in two-door or four-door saloon styles. It was probably just as well that Ford had largely lost interest in building convertibles, as the chassis was not really strong enough to cope with such coachwork without substantial strengthening. With a weight of 711 kg (14 cwt) and a 0–80 km/h (0–50 mph) acceleration time of around 34 seconds, the Model Y had respectable performance and its 105 km/h (62 mph) maximum speed was nothing to be ashamed of. Moreover, the fuel consumption, at 7 1/100 km (40 mpg), would disgrace many similarly conceived cars nearly 50 years later.

The Model Y was immediately popular with car buyers, over 39 000 examples being manufactured in 1933, a year in which only 55 000 cars were built at Dagenham altogether. This not only brought Ford of Britain back from the brink of disaster, but it established the company as one of the big three, in terms of sales, a position which Perry and his staff had long been trying to achieve. By 1934, the Y held 54 per cent of the British market for cars of under 9 hp, but there was a cloud on the horizon in the shape of the Morris Eight, launched in September of that year and an obvious copy at a lower price.

Ford took a leaf out of the Morris book and reduced the price of the Model Y not once, but twice. Finally, at the Ford Exhibition of 1935, the company announced that from now on there would be a basic two-door model, known as the Popular. The price quite took the breath away from the watching audience, and rightly so because this was the first – and only – time that a full four-seat saloon had been offered for so little. Although profit margins were cut to the bone, the trick worked; sales picked up so rapidly that the loss of revenue was more than made up by increased volume. In the early part of 1935 the

A four-seat drop-head coupé of 1933, with coachwork by Lambert of Kingston.

Y's share of the market had dropped to around 22 per cent, but the following year it had climbed back up to nearly double that.

Several slightly different versions of the Model Y were built at Ford plants around Europe, but the basic model remained remarkably unchanged during its life. Minor alterations took place, such as the addition of a second windscreen wiper, but sales remained good enough not to force major 'improvements' upon the company. After only 5 short years, when an amazing 157 668 cars had rolled off the production lines, the Y was withdrawn in favour of a new 8 hp model, the Ford 8, with more modern appearance and more streamlined body. Good as the new car might have been, however, it was the Model Y which set a whole new successful style for Ford and introduced a great many people to the joys of motoring.

FORD V8

Ford's Model A, which replaced the ubiquitous Model T in 1927, was a best-seller,
despite the 6-month pause between the
withdrawal of the T and the birth of the new
model. In 1930 the 4 millionth Model A left
Highland Park, in Detroit, which was more
significant than perhaps it seems, since the USA
was suffering in the depths of the Depression.
However, sales did start to decline during 1931,
but this time Henry Ford was ready, with a
successor well in hand.

Ford was renowned for his dislike and distrust
of the six-cylinder engine, a feeling which had
grown in him since the failure of the six-cylinder
Model K in 1906. He had vowed that he would
never make another six, but on the other hand
Chevrolet's new International was six-cylinder-
powered and, since this was in direct competition
with the Model A, he wanted to better it. His
decision was to make an eight-cylinder unit,
more specifically a V8. This would not be the first
such engine, but it would be the first to be fitted
to a mass-market motor car; as always, Ford
intended to give the people what they longed to
have (or what they thought they longed to have)
at a price they could afford.

The Ford empire already had a V8 engine, in
the shape of the unit used by the company's
Lincoln division, but this was very expensive to
produce, mainly because its cylinders were cast
separately from its crankcase. Henry was firmly
convinced that the only way to produce a V8 at a
reasonable price was to make the whole block-
and-crankcase assembly in one piece, but this
was said to be impossible by engineers who had
worked on such projects before. In typical style,
Henry declared that this was rubbish and set a
team of designers to work to solve the problems.

By May 1930, the first experimental engine
was complete, along the lines of Ford's proposal;
this then underwent many months of testing in
order to establish that it would be efficient and
reliable.

One of the difficulties lay in finding a design
which would be suitable for mass production: it

*The bodywork of the Ford V8 was quite
streamlined by 1935, when this four-door saloon
was manufactured.*

was one thing being able to hand-build a superb power unit, but it was another to adapt it for manufacture on a moving production line. Thirty different engines were constructed and fitted to Model A chassis for trials, but the old man was happy with none of them, so in December of 1931, 19 months after the first prototype had been put together, the President rolled up his sleeves and took personal charge of the project. He worked like a Trojan, and it should be remembered that by this time he was 68 years old, until he and his team finally arrived at a package which was acceptable to him. This feat was made the more remarkable by the fact that, at the same time, he was devoting much of his attention to the new Model Y for Great Britain; these were, perhaps not surprisingly, the last two cars in the design of which the great man took an active part.

The final production engine had a capacity of

3.6 litres and a 90° included angle between the cylinder banks, which, incidentally, were cast in unit with the crankcase, as Henry had demanded. The side-mounted valves were operated directly by a single camshaft located in the centre of the vee, which meant that the exhaust manifolds had to take a tortuous route between the cylinder banks to join up with the pipes. The crankshaft was suspended in only three bearings and the power output of the unit was quoted as 65 bhp.

Even for the production cars, the new engine was fitted to a modified Model A chassis, which really was not up to the sort of power being produced. A single-dry-plate clutch joined the motor to a three-speed gearbox with syn-

As on previous Ford models, the Tudor saloon, such as this 1932 two-door, was the popular version.

chromesh on the upper two ratios and a propeller shaft, enclosed in the fashionable torque tube, fed the drive from there to the live rear axle via a spiral-bevel final drive unit.

Suspension on the separate pressed-steel chassis was as crude as the chassis itself, with transverse leaf springs and radius arms at each end, and with a beam axle at the front. Lever-arm hydraulic dampers were the one bodily concession to the modern world. Braking was still enacted by means of rods, while others had long been using hydraulic systems, but at least brakes were fitted to all four wheels.

Announced on 31 March 1932, the V8, which in Ford parlance was known as the Model 18, even had the basic body styles of the Model A; most importantly, though, it was on offer for only a little more than the Model A had cost. The Press loved the car, being astounded by its performance, although it was suggested that one should treat the V8 with great respect on anything other than a straight, open road. With a power output of 65 bhp and a weight of only just over 1 tonne for the roadster, the new machine really did give an exhilarating ride: the maximum speed was 129 km/h (80 mph) and the car could reach 80 km/h (50 mph) in only 12 seconds, an acceleration figure which would not be disgraced by much more recent sports cars. No report had anything but praise for the new engine, its smoothness and lack of fuss being mentioned as frequently as its actual power. One road test pointed out that the gearbox was a joy to use, but followed this up with the comment that it was a shame that such a box should only come to light on a vehicle with so much torque that gearchang-

Visibility must have been somewhat restricted from this 1937 Dagenham coachbuilt coupé.

This 1936 fixed-head coupé was aimed at the more sporting-minded motorist.

ing was hardly ever necessary.

Henry Ford had hedged his bets when he plumped for a new V8, because alongside it he announced an updated four-cylinder car based very closely on the Model A. This car, which shared its new slanted radiator with the V8, was commonly known as the Model B, but Henry insisted that it be known as the improved Model A. In fact, he needn't have bothered to build it, because the public immediately clamoured to get its hands on the V8, which in any case was only marginally more expensive than its stablemate. By the end of the year, 298 647 V8s had been sold, compared with a figure of 133 539 for the Model B, and it is probable that, if it had not been for a difficulty in tooling-up to make the V8 in vast quantities, the B would have been a disaster. As it was, dealers who could not obtain enough V8s were suggesting that their customers switch to the Model B and were being successful in their efforts.

The company advertised the V8 as: 'The greatest thrill in motoring' and the public obviously agreed, because, as more cars became available, sales climbed rapidly. There were body styles to suit everyone – cabriolets, coupés, roadsters and convertible and fixed-head saloons –

and the cars were comfortably fitted out. Sales in 1933 amounted to 500 000 and by 1934 production was really well organised, with fourteen different styles of body available. Output took a real boost in that year when the Model 40 V8 replaced the original 18. This was a more modern car in terms of styling, but it still retained the rather inadequate chassis; nevertheless it sold well enough to encourage Ford at last to dispense with the four-cylinder Model B – although a four-cylinder car known as the B40 continued in Europe where the strange tax laws punished the V8.

On 19 June 1934, the 1 millionth V8 was manufactured and only a year later this figure had been doubled. By this time the Model 48 had been introduced, and this was endowed with a much stiffer chassis, together with modified suspension settings, which led to greatly improved handling. Indeed, the V8 was very successful in motor sport around the world, taking two victories in the Monte Carlo Rally and achieving many other sporting wins. A 2.2-litre

version of the car was also introduced in 1935, mainly with the British market in mind (cars were now being made at Dagenham), but this model, despite its smaller body, lost too much of its sparkle to be really successful and it was withdrawn in 1940.

Modifications from here on were legion, but mainly involved restyling of the bodywork to meet current fashion. Technically little was changed until the mechanical brakes finally gave way to hydraulics in 1939 and column change supplanted the original direct-acting floor-change a year later. After World War 1, the 1942 models were put back into production for several years, but in 1949 the old engine was transplanted into an all new body.

The V8 had always been a steady seller in Europe, being manufactured in Britain, France and Germany, and, apart from the small-engined version, styles had followed those of the parent country. It was therefore all the stranger that the most successful British V8 was announced in

The 1937 Ford V8 Club Cabriolet had only two seats, but provided practical transport.

1947, not long before the end of the line for that particular style in the USA. This model, famous as the Ford Pilot, used the pre-war Model 62 body, with a more powerful engine and a luxurious specification, which included such fittings as built-in hydraulic jacks, even though this particular car still offered hydraulic operation only for the front brakes. Over 22 000 Pilots were sold between 1947 and 1951, when it was replaced and a great many people were very sad to see it discontinued.

In fact the V8 had an enormous following the world over and a reputation for reliability which it thoroughly deserved. The V8 engine, which was the first of a long and unbroken line for Ford in America, was finally replaced by an overhead-valve unit in 1953, over 20 years after its introduction.

MG MIDGET (J2 TO TF)

The MG name, until the 1970s, was synonymous with fine sports cars; indeed, not even the interference of a chain of management teams at British Leyland could shake the faith of the masses of MG devotees in their beloved marque, with its famous octagonal symbol. By 1980, the Midget name was finally killed, but it nevertheless perpetuated the memory of a long line of distinguished machines made between 1929 and 1955 (the later cars were nothing but badge-engineered Austin-Healeys).

The first of this hallowed line was known as the M-type and was based very closely on the then-current Morris Minor. In fact, since Morris Garages was wholly owned by William Morris, who became Lord Nuffield in 1934, it is not surprising that the products of the MG Car Company, which Cecil Kimber founded and managed as a separate branch of Morris Garages, were all closely allied to Morris, and, later, Nuffield offerings. The M-type was exceedingly popular with enthusiastic drivers, but Kimber did not rest on his laurels. By 1930, he was already thinking about a new Midget, with racing particularly in mind.

He built a new chassis, with channel-section side members and tubular cross members, based closely on that of a French Rally that he owned. The most novel feature of this frame lay in the rear suspension, which as before made use of semi-elliptic leaf springs; the interesting point was that the rear end of each spring had rigid lateral location but was allowed to slide back and forth in a trunnion, rather than having a fairly flimsy shackle. The engine was flexibly mounted so that it would not be caused to twist, something which was a problem in the M-type, manifesting itself as a leaking rear main bearing oil seal; the radiator was mounted to the engine, so that the two moved in the chassis as a unit.

The prototype chassis was destined for a famous record-breaker, known as EX120, which George Eyston drove to exceed 161 km/h (100 mph) for the first time with a 750cc engine. It subsequently took many more records in Captain

The J2 Midget of 1932 was the first of the purpose-built roadsters and was hailed as simple yet beautiful.

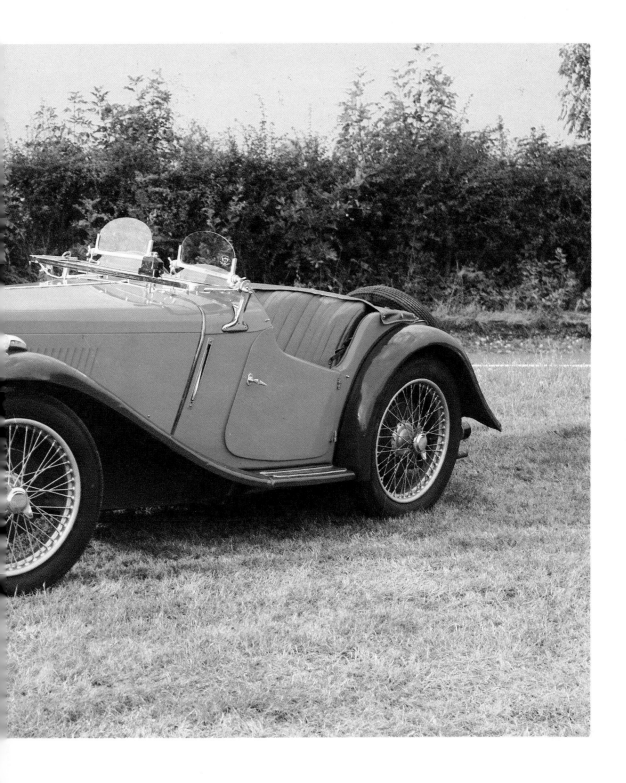

Eyston's capable hands. EX120 was followed by a new racer, called the Montlhéry Midget, which was available in supercharged or unsupercharged form. This had to be readied very quickly for the Brooklands Double 12 race in 1931 and fourteen cars were actually built in as many days. This exercise was worthwhile, however, because the Montlhéry took the first five places in the event.

By this time, Kimber felt that a new production Midget was due. The M-type engine had undergone a great deal of development, now having a cross-flow head to allow space for twin carburettors, and the new chassis had been seen to be a considerable improvement on the old one. His new J2 Midget, introduced in August 1932, caused enthusiasts to catch their breath with its beautifully, but simply, styled bodywork. This body, with its cutaway doors, folding windscreen and cycle wings, was extremely functional, in a sporting way, but it was also very well proportioned and truly elegant. It was styled by engineers rather than artists and yet it formed the basis for all the other Midget bodies – and indeed many others – until 1955.

The J2's chassis was very much the same as that of the Montlhéry, and the power unit was closely based on that of the M-type, with the racing modifications mentioned. It was an 847cc version of the 750cc racing unit, with a single overhead camshaft, four water-cooled cylinders and only a two-bearing crankshaft. Even in production form it managed to turn out a very healthy 36 bhp, aided by its twin SU carburettors.

A single-dry-plate clutch joined the engine to a four-speed 'crash' gearbox, which, for the skilled driver, was a joy to use, with its remote-control change. An open propeller shaft transmitted the power to the live rear axle by means of a spiral-bevel final drive unit.

Rear suspension was as mentioned earlier, while semi-elliptic leaves were also utilised at the front to locate the beam axle. Braking was taken care of by cable-operated drums all round and steering was dependent on a Marles-Weller unit. Wire wheels were standard fittings.

Although the two-bearing engine was quite sturdy, it could not cope with the maximum speeds of which it was capable. *The Autocar* had obtained just over 129 km/h (80 mph), which

Kimber had decreed their car should be capable of, so this compression ratio was lowered for production builders. Owners then complained that their cars were not as good as those of *The Autocar*.

The J2 was priced very reasonably and there was also a four-seat open or closed version, called the J1, which was slightly more expensive. The Midgets sold very well indeed and the company kept up its image with a further string of successes on the tracks and in record-breaking. For the 1933 London Motor Show, the J1 was dropped and its sister acquired swept wings; sales of the J2 continued to go well, with 2083 finally reaching buyers, but MG generally, despite its racing success, was not as prosperous as it should have been.

Sir William Morris told Cecil Kimber that he should restrict racing as much as possible from now on and buy as many components as possible from the Morris group. A new Midget was already on the stocks, however, and the J2 was withdrawn in January 1934 in preparation for the announcement of the improved P-type in March. This had a strengthened chassis, with a longer wheelbase (by about 3.8 cm or 1½ in) but the same track as before. The 20.3 cm (8 in) brake drums were enlarged to 30.5 cm (12 in), which brought the braking up to scratch, and Bishop cam steering was incorporated. Perhaps most importantly, a third crankshaft bearing was added to the engine and this made it stronger and smoother running. Power output was slightly down, at 35 bhp, but the engine could stand more tuning than previously. The whole transmission system was improved, although synchromesh had not been added to the gearbox. Body styling was just about the same as that of the J2, but comfort had been enhanced and there was more room inside. Prices were still very reasonable. In addition to these, a handsome coupé, known as the Airline, was offered as a standard option and many other special bodies were available from other coachbuilders.

Joined in the range by the N-type Magnette, the Midget helped MG to pick itself up, the PA, as it subsequently became known, reaching nearly 2000 owners. Apart from being a fine road car, the PA was very successful in competition and the Q-type racer soon followed it, with over

A 1935 MG PA; this had many improvements over the earlier J2.

The 1939 TB Midget was short-lived due to the outbreak of war, giving way to the legendary TC in 1945.

The 1953 TF was the black sheep of the family, considered by the MG faithful to be too soft.

100 bhp from the same old 750cc engine, albeit supercharged, and a pre-selector gearbox. The R-type racer, which came out in April 1935, was all new, with a new chassis and torsion-bar independent suspension all round. This was not a success and in mid-season the company withdrew from racing altogether.

This decision was certainly influenced by the fact that, in July, Lord Nuffield sold MG to Morris Motors and appointed Leonard Lord as Managing Director, in place of Cecil Kimber. Morris had never been keen on racing and this was seen as confirmation of that fact.

Nevertheless, the roadgoing Midgets continued to gain strength on the market and, in August, the slightly modified PB replaced the PA. This had its engine bored to 939cc, to give over 43 bhp, and it had a closer-ratio gearbox. There were still plenty of unsold PAs at this time, and they were offered at a vastly reduced price; however, they still were not wanted and, at the end of the year, the last twenty-seven were updated to PB specification. The PB itself only survived until early the following year, but in that time over 500 found homes.

The new TA Midget was not at all popular with MG enthusiasts, for it was considered to be a soft car. It had basically the same chassis, with some box sections in place of earlier channels, but it was a larger car, with the wheelbase lengthened by 16.5 cm ($6\frac{1}{2}$ in) and the track widened by 7.6 cm (3 in). It was granted that there was more room for people and luggage in the TA, but the beloved overhead-cam engine had been replaced by a 1292cc pushrod unit, producing 52 bhp, based on that of the Wolseley 10. All but the first few cars had synchromesh on all but first and reverse gears and a wet-cork clutch took the place of the dry one of the earlier models. Worst of all, the mechanical brakes had given way to hydraulics, which Cecil could never bring himself to trust.

The TA looked almost the same as the PB, but true MG followers did not take to it at first; the exhaust was even made noisier to give the TA a note of authenticity. Fortunately the fans were not all that stubborn and they seen realised that their fears were unfounded: the TA went very well and was almost certainly the best Midget yet, especially considering its price. An Airline coupé was offered at first, but this was soon replaced by a cheaper Tickford-bodied version; the four-seater was finally dropped for good.

3000 TAs were sold before the TB came on to the market early in 1939, not that the public realised that the TB existed until it was withdrawn at the outbreak of war in September. The only difference here was that a Morris Ten-derived 1250cc engine had replaced the TA's and a new dry clutch had been fitted. Despite the reduction in capacity, the new power unit produced over 54 bhp.

During World War 2, car production ceased completely and Cecil Kimber was finally sacked altogether. The factory turned out anything from trucks to bomber aircraft cockpits, but not a single car. At the end of the hostilities, the company concentrated on one model only at first, and this was the Midget, chosen because it was the only MG to sell more than 1000 a year before the War.

The short-lived TB gave way to the legendary TC, which was little changed, except for having conventional rear springs and new dampers. The body was the same basic shape as ever, but it was wider and gave more room for the passengers. Introduced in 1945, a total of 10 000 TCs had been made by the time it gave way to the TD at the end of 1949. What is more, a great many of these were exported, at a time when people in Britain could not obtain or afford petrol.

The TD was a very different Midget: the chassis was adapted from that of the Y-type saloon, with the rear axle slung under it, and it

had the luxuries of rack-and-pinion steering and coil-and-wishbone independent front suspension. Unfortunately, the distinctly unsporty Y-type disc wheels had to be used with the suspension arrangement, and these were not popular; they were also smaller than previous ones, which lowered the overall gearing (a hypoid-bevel final drive was new, as well). Again the body had been widened and it had a much more squat appearance than previously – lower and more streamlined. It handled well and it was comfortable to ride in. What is more it was just as fast as the TC, despite a substantial increase in weight. Purists did not like it at all, but that did not stop it easily outselling the TC, at nearly 30 000 in its 4-year life.

In 1952, a brand new successor to the TD was turned down by BMC, the new bosses of the Nuffield Corporation, on the grounds that they had a competitive Austin-Healey on the stocks, to which they wanted to give the go-ahead (the 100). The TD therefore struggled on, eventually being given a facelift in 1953. The TF had an even sleeker body line, with a sloping radiator grille, and its headlamps were now built into the front wings. It thankfully had new hubs to take wire wheels once again and it had the same engine as the Mark II version of the TD (slightly tuned at 57 bhp).

It was felt that the TF, which was finally announced at the 1953 London Motor Show, was not as good a car as the old TD and it was generally rejected by the enthusiasts. Although the 1500cc edition of the engine was offered eventually, this did nothing by way of appeasement and sales of the two versions up to 1955 were a modest 9600. The grand old lady had finally lost her teeth, after nearly 25 years and over 57 000 examples. The new MGA was a fine car, but it was in a completely different mould from its predecessor.

The Midgets may not have sold in millions, but they made the sports-car experience available to nearly anyone who could afford a car at all and they were certainly some of the best-known and best-loved sports cars ever.

MORRIS EIGHT

William Morris made several attempts at building a baby family car during the 1920s, but for one reason or another none was a real success; apart from anything else, they were never quite good enough to take on the impressive opposition of the day from companies such as Ford, Austin and Hillman. Without doubt, the most popular, and therefore the most profitable, of these was the little overhead-camshaft Minor of 1928, which for a number of important reasons is noteworthy today. Without it, the MG name may not have commanded the reverence that it does, for it was on the original Minor that the first MG Midget, the M-type, was based; this was the start of a long and famous line, which was still a major force fifty years later. Morris, knighted in 1929, contrived to produce an economy version of the Minor for 1932, in a standard battleship grey, with black radiator and lights, and he astounded the motoring Press and public alike by selling it for only £100 – the first full-sized car ever at that price. The threat of this announcement had caused Clyno to reduce their prices drastically in an attempt to make their own £100-machine in 1928 and, in doing so, they bankrupted themselves.

Despite all this, the Minor was not all that it might have been and sales of the cheap version were very disappointing. Despite the fact that the last cars were very well equipped, they could not compete with Ford's Model Y, which was altogether more modern, with more room inside, better performance and the same RAC horse-power rating (for tax purposes) for less money. The company therefore needed a new car to put it back on top of the lists; although it was cataloguing a fair range of cars, none was a best-seller and Morris was by now becoming rather bored with his empire and was concentrating on 'specialising', or buying up various outside suppliers.

The Morris approach to the problem was to copy: there is little doubt that the new Morris Eight, announced in September 1934, was a blatant crib of the Ford Model Y in terms of appearance. Under the skin, however, the little Morris had several distinct advantages over its

In 1947, when this four-door Series E saloon was made, the Morris Eight bore scant resemblance to its forebears.

Dagenham rival. First of all, semi-elliptic springs were used all round, rather than the somewhat wayward transverse leaf springs still pervading on the Ford front end. In addition, the Eight had excellent hydraulic brakes, as had Morrises for many years previously, while the Y still struggled to stop by mechanical commands. The double box-section frame was a considerable improvement on the flimsy Ford item and, despite being drilled for lightness, allowed an open body to be fitted without further strengthening; in fact the only drawback with drilling the chassis was that water could enter the box sections and bring on major rust.

Everything about the car was straightforward but effective. The engine was a side-valve straight-four with a capacity of 918cc and a compression ratio of only 5.8:1 (which allowed it to run on the cheapest petrol available); it had three main bearings, as opposed to the two of the Minor, and the carburettor and electric fuel pump came from SU, which company was by now part of the Nuffield Organisation.

Although the Minor had been fitted with a four-speed, synchromesh gearbox, Morris copied Ford again here and made do with three ratios, the top two being synchronised. The ratios were widely spaced, but were useful, particularly as second gear was just right for 48 km/h (30 mph) cruising. Gearchange was effected by means of a long, centrally mounted 'pudding-stirrer', which required only that a driver remember carefully that he did not have a fourth gear, as it was possible to find reverse by mistake. An open propeller shaft and a spiral-bevel final drive transmitted drive to the live rear axle, fabric universal joints being employed on the prop shafts of the early cars.

Wire wheels and Bishop cam steering completed the external mechanical picture, while bodywork came in two-seater, tourer and two-and four-door saloon form, the saloons being available with a sliding sunshine roof and two-tone paintwork. The 6-volt electrics were standard, as was an electric wiper, which was unusual

A Series I two-seater, with easy-clean wheels not really made standard until the advent of the Series II.

for the time. Prices were very reasonable. A 254 kg (5 cwt) van was also listed, as was a bare rolling chassis.

Inside, the car was even more roomy than the Model Y and it set a trend by exchanging the positions of the centre accelerator pedal and the right-hand brake pedal. Instrumentation was generous, but the dials themselves, mounted in the centre of the dash, were tiny. A futuristic steering column control stalk was used to look after lamp-dipping, horn and semaphore indicators (standard on saloons and extra on other styles). Interestingly, the indicators were not of the self-cancelling variety, but tiny mirrors mounted in the screen corners allowed the driver to check whether the arms were out or not.

The Eight was immediately well received by the Press, for it performed quite well and had cornering and stopping capabilities to match. The 23½ bhp engine gave the car a top speed of nearly 96 km/h (60 mph) and a fuel consumption of 7 l/100 km (40 mpg) or more, while the hydraulic dampers and the large drum brakes made it easy to handle. Sales took off immediately and 10 000 Eights had been delivered by early 1935; indeed, figures were so impressive that Ford were pushed into reducing the price of the

The Series II of 1938 was best distinguished from its predecessors by its painted radiator shell.

Model Y Popular to compete.

In mid 1935, Morris decided to have no more yearly model changes; instead, they introduced the 'Series' system, so that every car in the range became a Series I, II etc .... June saw the announcement of the Series I Morris Eight (the earlier versions have since been known as pre-Series cars), with very few alterations. Some changes, such as repositioning of the indicators had already been carried out, but the Series I acquired Hardy-Spicer couplings in place of the fabric joints in the propeller shaft and the word Eight on the radiator was replaced by a figure '8'.

Sales went from strength to strength and July of 1936 saw the 100 000th Morris Eight roll off the Cowley production line. In the 3 years up to 1937, no less than 20 000 tourers alone were sold and this fact prompted other manufacturers, who had quietly dropped the idea of open bodies for their products, to reconsider.

The Series II Eight came in 1938, although the van continued in Series I form until the end of the following year. In fact, very little was changed for

the new model: apart from new 'easy-clean' pressed-steel wheels, which in any case had found their way on to late Series I examples, the modifications were purely cosmetic. The real change came a year later with the streamlined Series E.

Although Morris had had things very much their own way for some time, sales began to drop with the Series II, in the face of more modern opposition, but the company was not to be outdone. The Eight underwent a dramatic facelift and emerged at the 1938 London Motor Show with a much sleeker body, fitted with a boot for the first time, faired-in headlamps and a smart curved radiator grille. The engine was beefed up at the same time and its power output boosted to $29\frac{1}{2}$ bhp; this, coupled with a new four-speed gearbox, improved acceleration figures enormously, while the car's remarkable economy remained. Inside, everything was new, including the new, more sensible but less interesting, instrument layout, situated in front of the driver. The removal of the running boards did far more than smooth the appearance of the Series E, of course; it added many inches to the interior dimensions, thus leaving plenty of room in the

One of the early Morris Eights, a 1935 pre-Series four-door saloon.

back for burly adults. Tourers were still listed, but by now the two- and four-seat cars shared the same body shell and it is doubtful whether any two-seat Series Es were ever made.

The Series E continued in production, joined in 1940 by the updated Series Z van, until 1948, and in fact the van was not discontinued until an amazing 5 years after that. Manufacture stopped during World War 2, but the Eight was changed remarkably little when production resumed. The tourer had gone from the range, four-doors and sun no longer went hand in hand and you could have any colour so long as it was black, but otherwise everything was as before.

The Morris Eight has often been criticised as mundane and suitable only for non-drivers, yet it found friends in all walks of life and it found a great many of them. The Series E boosted flagging sales and the $\frac{1}{4}$ million mark was passed at the end of 1938. By the time this fine old machine was ousted by (Sir) Alec Issigonis' fine new Morris Minor, 340 000 had left the line.

FIAT 500 'TOPOLINO'

The Italian firm of Fiat nearly entered the 'baby car' market in 1919, with their first type 500, but, although this was exhibited in 1918, Giovanni Agnelli decreed that the world was not yet ready for such a vehicle, so the car never reached the showrooms. It was, as it turned out, another 17 years before Fiat finally took the plunge, again with a type 500, but this time a completely different car, popularly known as the 'Topolino' or 'Mickey Mouse'.

It was 1934 when Agnelli, still firmly holding the Fiat reins, decided that a new utility car was needed and set two designers, Franco Fessia and Dante Giacosa, to work on the project. They started with a clean sheet of paper, the brief being to build a car which would appeal to all classes of people, particularly to those who had previously relied on their own feet or a horse and cart for transport. By 1936 the job was done and the result was a smart little two-seater, announced in April of that year.

The 'Topolino' was an immediate success. It compared favourably in price with the competition, such as the primitive Austin Seven, while offering much more refinement. If anything the key to its success lay in the fact that Giacosa and Fessia had insisted on building a miniaturised version of a full-sized car, rather than making 'cheap' synonymous with 'crude'; the 'Topolino' was also the first really new baby car since the Austin Seven, which, by 1936, was 14 years old. Such niceties as a four-speed synchromesh gearbox and really effective hydraulic brakes made the 500 not just a people's car, but a driver's car and, because of this, it soon became popular with housewives, for shopping, and with 'off-duty' racing drivers, for fun.

The basis of the 'Topolino' was a cross-braced pressed-steel chassis, which was peppered with judiciously drilled holes in order to make it as light as possible. The two-seat body was also of pressed steel and inspiration for its streamlined nose was apparently drawn from the contemporary Fiat 1500; the whole was an attractive creation which was available in closed or roll-top

The 500C was announced in 1949; it retained the B's overhead-valve engine and had a full-width grille.

form. There was no boot, as such; simply a shelf behind the seats, which could carry luggage, children or, at a pinch, a third adult. Strangely, direction indicators were only offered as an extra, but they were fairly desirable because the sliding windows, just like those of the more recent Mini, made hand signals a hobby for the double-jointed only.

A four-cylinder engine was fitted, consistent with the 'big car in miniature' idea; this side-valve unit was water-cooled and had a capacity of only 569cc, from which an output of 13 bhp at 4000 rpm was extracted. It was mounted well forward in the front engine compartment, which meant not only that the radiator could be mounted above and behind it but that it left room for long legs (despite an overall length of only just over 3.2 m [10½ ft], the driving position was comfortable for much more than the average short-legged Italian). The position of the radiator, just ahead of the passengers, rendered a heater unnecessary. The remarkably modern synchromesh gearbox was mounted in unit with the engine and it drove the rear wheels through a propeller shaft, a spiral-bevel final drive and a live rear axle.

Front suspension was advanced, too, consisting of a transverse leaf spring and wishbones, while quarter-elliptic leaf springs and radius arms located the rear axle. Hydraulic dampers were fitted all round. This suspension, combined with the excellent brakes and the location of the large 38 cm (15 in) wheels at the four corners of the car, made the 'Topolino' a delight to handle; road tests showed that there was hardly any body roll and that stability under braking was superb.

Unfortunately, the 500 did not go as well as it cornered and stopped – which is perhaps not surprising with only 13 bhp on tap. With an all-up weight of 533 kg (10½ cwt) it could manage a respectable 80 km/h (50 mph) or so, but it took nearly a quarter of a minute to reach 48 km/h (30 mph). Because of this somewhat stately acceleration, some drivers succumbed to the temptation to be over-enthusiastic in the gears, with the common result, with the rather low third ratio, of a broken two-bearing crankshaft.

If it was not fast, the 'Topolino' was certainly economical. At worst the fuel consumption would rise to around 7 1/100 km (40 mpg), while in one famous 1936 run from Paris to Madrid a standard example of the breed consumed 3.6 1-/100 km (78 mpg).

Various items of tuning equipment were soon

offered for the car, which was also available as a Simca in France and an NSU in Germany. SIATA offered an overhead-valve conversion in Italy, to raise the power output to 19 bhp, while Victor Derbuel in Germany supercharged the NSU version. Several special-bodied variants were built by independent companies and these often had remarkable performance.

Although the 'Topolino' was basically a two-seater throughout its long life, a four-seater cabriolet was built especially for the British market in 1939 and made possible by the fact that the chassis had been lengthened in mid-1938 to accommodate semi-elliptic rear springs. With a numerically greater final-drive ratio, the four-seater managed to overcome its weight penalty and retain its excellent fuel economy, but it did not have the charisma of its forebear.

By the time World War 2 came, 83 266 of Fiat's own version of the 500 had been sold; in addition to this the French and German equivalents were both very popular – in fact the Simca Cinq, as the French car was called, was the cheapest car on the French market and was in great demand. Production of the 'Topolino' was

suspended for the duration of the War, but it was resumed in 1945, despite the ravages that had been wrought on the factories. The only drawback, and a very large one, was that the 1940 list price had rocketed by 250 per cent to a crippling level; worse still, post-war shortages in war-torn Italy gave rise to a black market price of about $2\frac{1}{2}$–3 times as much again. Nevertheless, sales did pick up again.

Modifications were few until the 500B appeared in 1948; in 1938 there were bigger brakes, a more powerful starter and, for Britain only, a new oil pump – in addition to the modified rear suspension mentioned. The B model was announced with a new, aluminium-headed pushrod engine, producing $16\frac{1}{2}$ bhp and boosting the top speed only slightly to 90 km/h (56 mph). This car also had a mechanical fuel pump to take the fuel from the dash-mounted tank (it had previously relied on gravity) and an additional torsion bar

A four-seat cabriolet, for Britain, was announced in 1939, but it lost much of the character of the 'Topolino'.

for the rear suspension.

21 000 of the 500Bs were sold in the model's life of only just over 1 year; the 500C took its place after being presented at Earl's Court, in London, in 1949. Apart from the addition of a heater, the alterations to this version were largely cosmetic: a full-width grille was added, as was an extended tail with a spare wheel locker and new rear lamps. Flashing indicators became standard equipment only 2 years later. Top speed had risen to 98 km/h (61 mph), still with exceptional economy, but the 'Topolino' lost ground to the opposition when it came to climbing hills.

A wood-trimmed estate car, the Giardinetta, had been launched alongside the series B and this continued to the end, but it shed its wood in 1951. This was the only four-seat 500 ever to be

The station wagon shed its wood in 1951, but continued in production until 1955 as the Belvedere.

generally available. Despite its lack of power, the 'Topolino' also achieved its share of competition success, in rallies, sprints and endurance events, winning an Index of Performance at Le Mans. It was even used as the basis of several early 500cc Formula Three cars.

By 1954, sales had dropped to a mere trickle, so the 500 was finally withdrawn in favour of the new 600 model. In the life of the classic 'Topolino', over 500 000 examples were made in Italy alone.

PANHARD DYNA

World War 2 saw most of the world's car production come to a complete standstill; this was particularly true in France, where the German occupation precluded anything but clandestine work. At the end of the War, Panhard realised that the time was ripe for a completely new type of car, one that would be cheap to buy and, far more importantly, cheap to run and maintain in those days of rationing and extraordinarily high prices of fuel, tyres and other motoring essentials.

They based their new car on a design of J. A. Grégoire, who had long been noted for his preference for front-wheel drive. He had been responsible for the Amilcar Compound, which had all-independent suspension, front-wheel drive and a unitary-construction body, which made considerable use of aluminium-alloy castings. The new design was in this spirit, ·but although it was intended to develop the machine in Great Britain and in Australia, Panhard took it over and toned down its ingenuity and originality just a little.

Despite the changes, the new Panhard was still revolutionary and it aroused a great deal of curiosity among the public, members of which were fascinated by this remarkable new machine. It began to sell very well shortly after its announcement in 1945, customers soon becoming used to the idea of a completely different type of Panhard.

Perhaps the most remarkable feature of the Dyna, as the latest car was called, was the fact that its otherwise conventional saloon body was built of aluminium alloy, not simply pressed, but, in the case of many parts, cast. This obviously added to the car's attraction, as it meant that the likelihood of corrosion problems was reduced to just about nil – something which was very important in those times of austerity.

The engine was a horizontally opposed, twin-cylinder unit, with a capacity of only 610cc. Once again aluminium alloy was used profusely in the engine's construction, the cylinders, which were in unit with their heads, being of that material, but being lined with cast iron. A single camshaft lay below the central, built-up crankshaft and it operated the overhead valves, which were in-

One of the original Dyna models, seen in Paris during the 1954 Monte Carlo Rally.

In 1954, the Dyna was completely restyled, but retained alloy panels.

clined in hemispherical chambers, via pushrods and rockers. Remarkably, the valves were closed by torsion-bar springs rather than the customary helical variety, a collar over the valve stem providing a purchase for the arm driven by each torsion bar. One of the advantages of such a system was that the valve could be made substantially shorter than if it had a helical spring and this, in turn, would reduce the mass of the valve and, indeed, the speed at which it would bounce on its seat. Tappet adjustment was also strange, in that one had to screw the rocker up or down its threaded pivot pillar, rather than carrying out an adjustment at its tip. Power output of this little air-cooled engine was around 15 bhp, which was quite respectable for the engine size at that period.

The first stage in the transmission process was a single-dry-plate clutch and this was mounted in unit with a four-speed gearbox, whose uppermost ratio was an overdrive. The gearchange lever was a strange device which protruded through the dashboard and formed a sort of column change. Unlike the original Grégoire design, the Panhard had been given rear-wheel drive, so an open propeller shaft took the drive backwards from the gearbox to a live rear axle, which it drove via a hypoid-bevel final drive unit and a differential.

The styling of the front-wheel-drive Dyna was subtly altered during the 1950s and early 60s.

Front suspension was by a curious twin-transverse leaf spring arrangement, while the rear was even more unusual, with torsion bars and radius arms. Lever-type hydraulic dampers were fitted all round and a rack-and-pinion unit took care of the steering. Hydraulic drum brakes were fitted at each wheel.

The wheels were particularly interesting, since they consisted of aluminium alloy rims bolted directly to the brake drums, without any other form of centre.

This initial version of the car was a great success, providing reliable transport for the hard-up French people, but it was soon improved by a change to a 32 bhp version of the engine, with a capacity of 750cc, which increased the performance somewhat. This was in 1950 and, only 2 years later, the capacity was increased to 850cc. By this time the engine had been made even more reliable by the incorporation of a novel hydraulic tappet arrangement in which hydraulic pressure took up any play in the valvegear by lifting the rocker pedestal; this was certainly unusual and it avoided the possibility, often present with such arrangements, of 'pump-up' occurring.

Sales continued unabated, but in 1954 came a bombshell, for Panhard decided to move the driven wheels of the Dyna to the front, with a consequent redesign of the whole car. This redesign was dutifully carried out and a new body was evolved – a body which evoked extremely

The cabriolet was one of several styles of Dyna body available in 1957.

mixed reactions from the critics, who either loved it or hated it. This body was still largely made of aluminium, although now castings had been dispensed with in the bodywork and pressings had taken their place.

Other than the fact that the rear axle was now a curiously shaped dead one and the gearbox was now part of a trans-axle, the mechanical parts of the Dyna were substantially unaltered. The standard car now had a power output of around 50 bhp, which was enough to move six people around at up to 129 km/h (80 mph) and yet return a fuel consumption of approximately 14 km/l (40 mpg), which said a great deal for the aerodynamics of the new body shape, bulbous or not. At this time, two- or four-door saloons were available in the Dyna range.

Sales continued to boom, output being plenty high-enough for the company, and improvements continued to be made. In 1957, the alloy body was ousted by a steel one, which may have been cheaper, but was heavier and gave in to rust rather easily.

1961 saw the advent of the smart little PL17 Tigre coupé, which offered a 60 bhp version of the engine, giving a maximum speed of over 145 km/h (90 mph). This was one of the Dynas which was particularly successful in competition, albeit

There was even an estate car version of the Panhard; this example was made in 1960.

in tuned form, and Panhard's competition success with the Dyna culminated in a Monte Carlo Rally win in 1961 (a win which was largely discounted by the competition at the time, since the rules had been changed – seemingly to favour the Dyna).

In 1964, the final versions of the Dyna appeared, these being the 24C two-door saloon and the 24CT sports coupé. These had sleeker styling once again, and a top speed of over 161 km/h (100 mph) – at last – which was extremely respectable for an 850cc engine. The CT had a shorter wheelbase than the C and it was more compact altogether, so its performance had a slight edge over that of its sister. Several other changes came in with the model 24s. For instance, the gearbox acquired synchromesh on all four forward gears and a long, vague floor-change supplanted the acceptable 'column' one.

The sporting potential of the Panhard Dyna was such that many firms began to build special bodies to go with the mechanical components and systems of the Dyna and many of these were extremely successful in competition. Various development cars were made after this, to incorporate the more successful aspects of the competition cars, such as five-speed gearboxes, disc brakes all round and 70 bhp, but these were never fully developed, as, in 1965, Panhard were formally taken over by the Citroën company, which had possessed a stake in the Panhard concern for 10 years or so.

By 1967, only the 24CT coupé was still being made, as the others had all been dropped. The remaining version had disc brakes all round, but it, too, was dropped from the catalogues only a little later. The Panhard Dyna had certainly carried out its task of satisfying the people – indeed it had probably exceeded expectations. What is more, it was good enough to remain in the showrooms, admittedly in rather different forms, for nearly 20 years.

RENAULT 4CV

During the years before World War 2, Renault were producing rather staid and mundane motor cars, but they were at least producing them in relatively large numbers, the factories turned out 250 cars every day. What is more, cars represented only one part of the company's diverse business, which included the manufacture of trucks, tractors, stationary engines, railcars and even aircraft, not to mention steel and the various accessories and components to go with or in their other products.

With around 40000 employees, the company was one of France's biggest employers, but Louis Renault, who had founded and built the concern, had never been renowned for his ability to deal diplomatically with people and this was a problem which seemed to grow as he aged. The Depression of the early 1930s had brought great unrest, despite the fact that the workers managed to retain their jobs, and this had led to a series of strikes, culminating in the workers occupying the factories in 1936. Renault handled all of this very ineptly and it left him feeling bitter towards the whole of the workforce and perhaps not too unhappy when the German army marched into Paris in 1940 and effectively put a stop to communism.

Despite the company's industrial relations problems, new cars were being planned and Louis Renault's visit to Germany in 1938 to cast an eye over the prototype KdF-wagen, which was to see light of day in 1945 as the Volkswagen, was very significant. He knew that this was the right sort of car for the people – a car that was efficient and practical, yet could be made at a price everyone could afford. He and his colleagues set to work straight away to plan a similar car, but progress though steady was slow and it was not until 1941 that the first drawings were finished.

By this time, war had intervened and France had fallen and Renault had a very difficult choice to make: he could refuse to cooperate with the German occupiers and see his empire either simply taken away from him or, worse still, decimated, or he could collaborate. In view of his

This 1959 Renault 4CV displays just how little the car changed during its long life.

*A great deal of secret work was done on the 4CV
during World War 2; this is the first prototype.*

troubles with the workforce and the fact that he
felt that the war was as good as lost, he, along with
many of the rest of France's industrial leaders,
chose the latter course. This allowed him
to go on producing as before, but more importantly gave him the opportunity to develop his
new people's car in secret. A great deal of work
was carried out on the new car at this time, but
prototypes could not be built and tested until
after the Liberation. In any case the Allies
bombed the Renault factories on many occasions,
believing that the company was manufacturing
tanks for the Germans, and a considerable
amount of time and effort went into rebuilding
after each occasion, which all hampered production and development work.

When the end of the War came, or more
accurately when France was liberated after D-
Day in 1944, Louis Renault was arrested as a
traitor and all his plans of being ready at the end

of hostilities with the right car for the moment
were for nothing. He was never tried, he was
simply beaten and broken, and only a month after
his arrest he died in prison. The new French
government then decided to nationalise the
Renault company, not really knowing how it was
going to cope with this giant, but feeling that this
was the right move to make. It appointed an
engineer, Pierre Lefaucheux to head the company and it was under his enterprising control
that the new baby car, planned so long ago by
Louis, was finally built, tested and announced.

Like Renault, Ferdinand Porsche was arrested
and imprisoned after the War, and it was felt that
it would be useful if one of his duties while a
prisoner was to be taken to Paris to inspect the

drawings of the new Renault; as the 'father' of the people's car, he ought to know if the company was going the right way or not. Porsche obviously did not suggest many changes, as prototypes were undergoing testing in Algeria only a short while after the War's end.

Lefaucheux was extremely impressed with the new car, so much so that he ordered it into production straightaway, simultaneously demanding that all other models be dropped from the range in its favour.

Technically, the Renault 4CV, as it was named, was very advanced, because it had a unitary construction body/chassis unit, using stressed steel panelling, rather than the currently popular rolling chassis with a separate bolted-on body unit. Apart from making construction simpler and cheaper, the unitary body/chassis offered much improved torsional rigidity over its predecessor, which in turn led to better handling.

The engine was an in-line four-cylinder unit of 760cc, which developed a modest 19 bhp in standard form. Overhead valves were operated by pushrods and rockers from a single camshaft mounted in the cylinder block and the crankshaft ran in three main bearings. The most interesting point about this useful little engine was that it was mounted in the rear of the car, behind the rear wheels, as in the Volkswagen; considering that, unlike the Volkswagen's power unit this had in-line cylinders, the rear overhang of the body was remarkably small.

A single-dry-plate clutch was mounted on the end of the crankshaft at the front of the engine and a short shaft then transmitted the power forwards past the spiral-bevel final drive unit into the three-speed gearbox, which itself was particularly unusual for having synchromesh on all three forward ratios. The gearbox and final drive were mounted in unit with each other and with the engine and clutch, the gearbox being ahead of the rear wheels.

Suspension was independent all round, another advanced feature, by means of double wishbones and coil springs at the front and universally jointed swinging axles at the rear. Hydraulic telescopic dampers were fitted all round. Drum brakes were used all round, and they were hydraulically operated, while a simple and efficient rack-and-pinion steering system

Prototype number 2 shows much greater similarity to the final production car.

took care of directional control. The wheels themselves were interesting, the centres being fixed to the hubs, while the rims were detachable; this seemed to be rather an old-fashioned system on such an otherwise advanced machine.

The body itself was considered ugly by most contemporary critics, but like that of the Volkswagen it was functional, having four proper seats and four doors. Fittings were by no means luxurious, but they were adequate, and there was a very reasonable amount of luggage space under what would normally have been the bonnet.

When the 4CV was announced at the 1947 Paris Motor Show, it attracted a great deal of interest and a great many orders. Production at first was slow, however, as the company tried to recover from the ravages of war: not only had the factories been bombed, but there were shortages of many of the materials needed in car manufacture, such as steel and rubber for tyres. Nevertheless, sales continued apace, the car quickly acquiring the nickname 'Cockchafer' or, due to the generous use of yellow ochre paint confiscated from the German Afrika Korps, 'Little Pat of Butter'.

Performance was excellent for such a small engine and such a low power output. Acceleration was slow, but the top speed of the 4CV was around 97 km/h (60 mph), which was more than enough to keep up with most of the other traffic. Fuel consumption was very frugal, too, something which was very important in post-war rationed Europe, and 7 l/100 km (40 mpg) could easily be reached.

1950 saw the 100000th car leave the production line, while, by 1954, the 1 million mark had been reached. Various minor changes were made to the car during its long life, perhaps the most significant being a reduction in capacity of the engine to 750cc in 1951 and the option of an automatic clutch in 1955. Styling never changed, although minor details were altered – items such as the side windows, whose opening arrangements were changed, and the wheels, which became more conventional.

Although the standard car remained utilitarian, sporting versions were made, with power

This is the first production 4CV; the car went on sale in 1947.

outputs of as much as 38 bhp and with this sort of specification the 4CV was quite successful in competition. What is more, the concept was further developed in 1956 to produce the 850cc Dauphine, which in its turn was enormously successful. Regardless of this, however, the 4CV continued in production until 1961, when it became the first French car to sell over 1 million. It was finally replaced by the still-current R4.

VOLKSWAGEN 'BEETLE'

It is strange to recall that the most popular motor car of all time arose like the proverbial phoenix from the ashes of Nazi Germany at the end of World War 2. It is nonetheless true, however, that the definitive 'people's car' was developed in order to fulfil a promise to all Germans by Adolf Hitler and to help to further his political career – although the latter was less widely publicised.

To trace the genesis of the Volkswagen – which literally means 'people's car' – it is necessary to look back to the grand Austro-Hungarian Empire, now Czechoslovakia, in 1875. This is where and when Ferdinand Porsche was born and it was his dream, one that persisted for many years, which finally brought about this legendary machine. Trained as an engineer, Porsche gained a doctorate and, in 1899, joined the Austrian Löhner company as an electrical engineer. In 1906 he was appointed Technical Director of Austro-Daimler and 10 years later he had reached the exalted position of Managing Director. It was while working with Austro-Daimler that his interest in small cars first came

to light, with the delightful little Sascha of 1921; after some internal argument, this 1097cc, in-line four-cylinder-engined machine was put into production a year later. It was a particular success in competition, its remarkably advanced 50 bhp, twin-overhead-camshaft power unit giving it a maximum of nearly 90 mph.

In 1923, Dr Porsche moved on to be Chief Designer and Technical Director of Daimler, where he was responsible for a line of successful and famous cars, and, after a spell back in Austria with Steyr in 1929, he set up his own design consultancy the following year in Stuttgart. His first project for himself was to lay down the preliminary sketches from a people's car, something which he had wanted but had not been allowed to build previously.

In 1931, the Zündapp motor cycle company commissioned him to build a prototype version of just such a car, which he did. This machine,

A four-wheel-drive prototype of 1937/8; note the shuttered military headlamps.

three examples of which were built, was powered by a 1200cc, five-cylinder radial engine, but Zündapp were not satisfied and they scrapped the idea. Another motor cycle manufacturer, NSU, then took up the challenge and this time Porsche developed a horizontally opposed, four-cylinder engine with air-cooling, which he fitted at the rear of the car. This 1448cc unit represented the first manifestation of the Volkswagen trademark to which the company remained firmly faithful for so many years. NSU were not entirely happy with the engine and they instructed their own Head of Design, Walter Williams Moore, to modify it. By the time this had been carried out to the satisfaction of the management and five prototypes had been constructed and tested at NSU's Neckarsulm factory, motor cycle sales had revived to such an extent that the company lost interest in the project. Fortunately, they returned the prototypes to Porsche, so that he could continue to work on them in his own time; the flat-four was not a new invention, having been used in several early cars and motor cycles, but Porsche and his assistants, Karl Rabe, Josef Kales and Frank Reimspiess, developed the concept to offer adequate power and economy combined with excellent reliability.

By 1934, Adolf Hitler had risen to power in Germany and Dr Porsche was very fortunate that the Chancellor considered him to be of sufficiently Aryan stock to be trusted and employed. Through the Reichsverband der Automobil Industry (Association of Motor Manufacturers), Hitler's government commissioned Porsche to build his long-dreamed-of people's car. Of course, the Doctor already had prototypes running around, so it did not take him long to construct three cars to a specification to suit Hitler. Indeed, at the 1935 Berlin Motor Show, Hitler said in his opening speech that, due to the brilliance of Porsche, it had been possible already to plan a new Volkswagen.

Those original prototypes, known as VW3, were equipped with a 985cc, overhead-valve version of the flat-four which, with a compression ratio of 5.6:1, produced a modest $23\frac{1}{2}$ bhp at

This 'Beetle' was made in 1947, the first year in which VWs were available to the general public.

3000 rpm. Exhaustive testing was carried out during 1936 (177 023 km [110 000 miles] being covered in only 2 months) and, by 1937, thirty protoypes, built for Porsche by Daimler-Benz, were in action, these not surprisingly being known as VW30. The final prototypes of the car, VW38, were built with either the 985cc power unit or a 704cc version of it.

Hitler made a speech to the public promising to make available to them a true people's car, one which everyone could afford to drive and would want to drive; what is more he said that his car would be within reach of most people's pockets, although the price was something over which the government and Dr Porsche found it difficult to agree. It seems that Hitler's real motive for wanting to build such a car was that it would keep money in Germany and that it would be easily and cheaply adaptable for military use in the conflict which, by then, he was expecting.

During the 1950s the rear window was enlarged, but styling was otherwise little changed.

In 1937, the Chancellor founded the Gesellschaft für Vorbereitung des Deutschen Volkswagens (Association for the Manufacture of the German People's Car) and on 26 May of the following year, he laid the foundation stone of a new factory at Fallersleben, 80 km (50 miles) east of Hamburg. This complex was known as Kraft durch Freude Stadt (Strength through Joy Town), being titled after Hitler's organisation of that name, which was largely responsible for the project. Indeed, in 1938, the car was officially dubbed the KdF-wagen and the company Volkswagenwerk GmbH. By the end of the year, advance orders for nearly 170 000 cars had been taken and many payments were made in anticipation of an early delivery; in fact, it was this money which largely financed the new factory.

Unfortunately, production was not to be – for a few years at least – as Hitler decided he would rather like to own Poland, but the design was quickly modified for military use. Two versions were produced: the cross-country Kubelwagen and the amphibious Schwimmwagen, which had the added luxury of four-wheel drive. Both were equipped with an 1131cc version of the engine, which produced only a little more power at 25 bhp, but considerably more torque. Over 70 000 of these were manufactured during the hostilities and the Kubelwagen has been extremely popular ever since, even prompting 'kit-car' copies.

The factory was devastated by bombing, but military production continued until the end. It was the US Army which reached the town first, in April 1945, and it was not long before its name was changed to Wolfsburg to exclude any Nazi connections. When control of the country was divided between the occupying powers, Wolfsburg fell into British hands and there it remained until military rule ceased in 1949. Under the British, rebuilding began and the first production cars left the factory. In 1945 and 1946, all the cars manufactured went to the Army, 1785 in 1945 and an astounding 10 020 in the following year. By this time the 1131cc engine had been standardised and it characterised Porsche's lifetime philosophy that it was best to have a large engine in a low state of tune, so that it could be run at full speed for long periods without any problems.

In these early machines, synchromesh was unheard of and brakes were operated by cables, but the VW was extremely reliable and exceptionally cheap. Everything about the vehicle was basic – simple torsion bar suspension was just another example – but it worked. There was only one 'standard' specification, the only luxury being a choice of colour, but this did not detract from the car's popularity. 1947 saw the first fifty-six exports and by May of the following year 25 000 Volkswagens had been built. By this time, Heinrich Nordhoff had become General Manager and, under his guidance, the company flourished to the extent that the factory was being expanded by the end of the decade.

The convertible has always been a popular model and can fetch high prices secondhand.

The 1303S of 1973 was a limited-edition model, with extras such as wide wheels.

In 1949, an export version of the 'Beetle' – never an official title – was in production, with a slightly improved specification, and the first US orders were received. All the cars had in common poor roadholding, low performance, almost non-existent styling, a lack of luggage space and not particularly comfortable seating and yet they had a certain appeal which transcended all this. Their rugged reliability, coupled with an incredibly long life, has always made Volkswagens extremely attractive all over the world.

Radical changes have never been made to the 'Beetle', although there has been a policy of steady improvement. 1954 saw the engine enlarged to 1192cc, with 30 bhp on tap, while 1960 brought a stronger engine and another 4 bhp. Synchromesh was also adopted during this period, as were hydraulic brakes, which improved the car considerably. Styling changes were equally steady, the split rear window disappearing and the new one growing larger, but the basic shape of the car remained completely unchanged.

In 1961, a 45 bhp, 1493cc engine was offered, as was a special Karmann-Ghia coupé body (a cabriolet had been listed by that styling house in 1949). Several different body variations have been tried over the years, usually using the same floor pan and running gear, but none has been nearly so successful as the 'Beetle' and all have been outlived by it. In fact, part of the beauty of the car is the fact that its semi-stressed body bolts on to a separate braced floor pan which has been widely employed by beach buggy and 'special' builders.

1963 saw the 54 bhp 1500S, 1965 a new 1285cc, 40 bhp engine and 1966 a very important change from 6-volt to 12-volt electrics – until this time, the headlamps had been little better than candles. Sales continued apace until the end of the 1960s, 1955 having seen the 1 millionth VW leave the production line and 1969 the 15 millionth. After this, popularity began to wane, however, despite the introduction of several new models, such as the 1300 and 1302S and the 1600. Automatic transmission had been made available in 1968 and the torsion-bar front suspension was replaced by a MacPherson strut system in 1970 (the rear remained dependent on swinging axles, trailing arms and torsion bars). Above all the legendary reliability and unburstability of the car were still strong features.

In 1972, the Volkswagen finally passed the all-time record of the Ford Model T, when on 17 February number 15 007 034 left the line. By then the car was being manufactured in plants all round the world, but orders were dwindling and the early 1970s finally saw the company forsake its traditions with the new front-engined K70, a design acquired with the NSU company. This proved to be the first of a whole new generation of VWs, but by the end of the decade, with over 20 million 'Beetles' under their corporative belt, Volkswagen were still continuing manufacture of their original people's car in several factories outside their native Germany. This all-time best-seller should perhaps provide a lesson for every mass producer of motor cars.

CITROËN 2CV

The 1930s saw the motor industry recovering from the Depression years and by the middle of that decade the ordinary motorist had a vast range of cars from which to choose. However, sales started falling as 1940 approached and the Munich crisis of 1938 set the seal on events by causing increased taxes to be levied, at least in Britain, in order to help the rearmament drive. Had it not been for the outbreak of World War 2 a year later, which all but halted car production for its duration, many manufacturers of luxury cars might well have been in serious trouble anyway.

Citroën was one of several European companies which recognised a need for a new small car, to enable even the most impecunious to become mobile. In 1936, Pierre Boulanger, then the company's general manager, and already with the famous *traction avant* system to his credit, outlined the concept of this new car, and work started straight away on detailed design and construction of prototypes. By 1939, there were 250 examples of this new Deux Chevaux, or 2CV, as it was to be called, ready for display at that year's Paris Motor Show. Sadly, the war prevented that exhibition ever taking place and Monsieur Boulanger's new baby ('Four wheels under an umbrella' he called it) was supposedly mothballed for the duration.

In fact, work continued in secret during the occupation of France, but it was not until 1948, nearly 10 years after its birth, that the Citroën 2CV finally went on sale. It was intended to fill the gap between the horse and cart and the full-size motor car and was thus extremely functional.

Every system in the car was simple yet effective. The body, while looking as though it might have been fashioned out of a discarded Nissen hut, was actually formed from very straightforward pressings, with a strong, but ugly, corrugated bonnet. Doors, bonnet and wings were quickly detachable for servicing or repair and the roof and boot cover comprised canvas sheets which rolled back to reveal the respective apertures. Even the seats were no more than hammocks, but there were four of them and four doors provided access.

Power came from a sturdy little 375cc, horizontally opposed, air-cooled engine, with pushrod-operated overhead valves. Even for such a small power unit, however, the power output was miserably small, at 8 bhp, and the top speed was therefore a mere 55 km/h (34 mph). Power was deliberately restricted, however, in order to prevent overloading of the vehicle – although this seems to have been a strange way of

By 1966 the 2CV had gained a rear quarter window and front-hinged doors.

This twin-engined, four-wheel-drive version was first produced in 1958, for off-road use.

going about achieving that end – but fuel consumption was correspondingly impressive, at around 4.3 l/100 km (65 mpg).

A remarkably modern four-speed gearbox transmitted the drive through a spiral-bevel final-drive unit to the front wheels. This box was all-indirect, top gear being in effect an overdrive, and synchromesh was fitted to all ratios. Equally advanced rack-and-pinion was standard, as were drum brakes all round, the front ones, unusually, being mounted inboard.

A novel form of interconnected suspension was introduced on the 2CV: nominally, the wheels were all independently sprung, on leading arms at the front and trailing arms at the rear, with inertia dampers and coil springs all round; however, the arms also acted each side on a common, longitudinally mounted, coil spring, located under the floor, so that when the front wheels hit a bump, the rear of the car would rise slightly in order to reduce pitching to a minimum. The roadholding of the car was – and is – very good, but the roll angles which this strange suspension system allows belie this and the spectacle of a 2CV cornering hard must have

The 1980 2CV6. Like most really successful cars, the 2CV changed very little in thirty years.

given many an approaching or following driver a heartstopping moment.

When Citroën's ugly duckling finally took to the roads in 1948 it was an immediate success with the public and it was not long before the company could not build enough cars to meet demand. Despite its lack of performance and its strange appearance, the latter not helped by the standard drab grey colour, the French people fell in love with the 2CV for its low price and its sheer practicality. 1950 saw 48 000 cars produced, while in the next year this figure rose to 78 000 as sales gained even greater momentum. Within a short time the company was turning out 1000 2CVs each day, but this was still not enough to satisfy demand.

The first change of any substance took place in 1954, when the engine capacity was increased to 425cc and the power output raised to a staggering 12 bhp. At the same time, a centrifugal clutch was made a standard fitting and a light van, equally freakish in appearance, joined the range. In 1958, a twin-engined, four-wheel-drive version of the

It was in 1954, when this car was made, that engine capacity was increased to boost power output to 12 hp.

2CV was introduced, with off-road use in mind, but this was not a great success and was short-lived.

Far more important were the steady minor developments carried out to the standard car over the years. In 1961, the somewhat more stylish Ami 6 was added to the 2CV family, using the same components, but having a 602cc version of the engine. This unit soon found its way into the standard car as well, this being known as the 2CV6, while the smaller engine continued in the 2CV4. The last of the 2CV's sisters was born in 1968, this being the Dyane, which used the 425cc engine and the usual mechanical components in a more-conventional four-door bodyshell.

A host of other changes have taken place over the years, the main one being that the body, despite retaining its original basic shape, is far

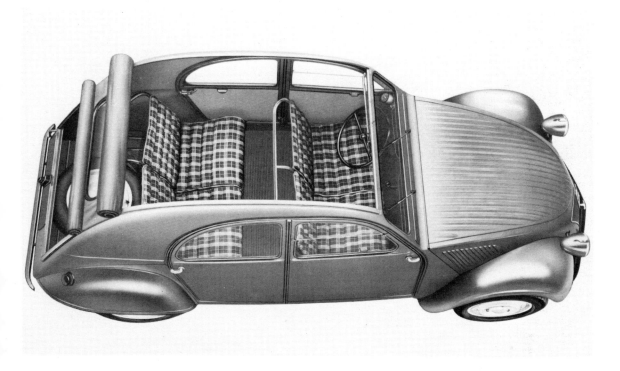

more pleasant to behold and is considerably less spartan in its fitting out. For all the updating, however, the 2CV has retained the same 'works' and with them all its character. It has completely defied fashion and its sales have gone from strength to strength in the fuel-crisis-ridden 1970s, after tailing off towards the end of the 1960s.

The 2CV has long enjoyed cult status in France, but, despite sales passing the $2\frac{1}{2}$ million mark in 1966, right-hand drive versions were not made until 1954 – and then only because the company realised the lengths to which the British people were going to buy and import to Great

The interior of the 1952 version was very basic, with hammock seats and roof and boot lid comprised of fabric covers.

Britain an old example. The car was very slow to catch on outside France, but young people began to buy them because they were cheap and they were reputed to be eminently reliable (which was probably just as well since spare parts were by no means abundant).

With sales at $4\frac{1}{2}$ million in February 1980, the 2CV is an anachronism, but it continues to flourish and it would undoubtedly lose much of its appeal were it to be completely modernised.

MORRIS MINOR

Unlike the vast majority of motor cars, the Morris Minor of 1948 was a product of a designer's mind rather than the end result of an interminable series of meetings, changes of mind and sundry committee decisions. Every motoring enthusiast, not to mention a large number of lay motorists, can remember without any effort that the now-cherished Morris Minor was the brainchild of Sir Alec Issigonis, even though he has since become far more famous for his legendary Mini.

Issigonis, who at that time had not received his knighthood, began work with Morris in 1936. His first design to see the light of day was the Series M Morris Ten, which was announced in 1939, just before the outbreak of World War 2. This was one of the first cars to make use of unitary construction, thereby doing away with the need for a chassis; otherwise, however, it was fairly conventional. At the same time, Issigonis was working hard on the design and manufacture of a lightweight racing car, known as the Lightweight Special, which he and his friend George Dowson finally completed in 1939 and subsequently raced with enormous success.

When war came, Issigonis stayed with Morris and devoted his time to designing odd devices for the army, most of which never reached production. However, he was not entirely idle as far as car development was concerned: he gave plenty of thought to ways of improving suspension design, which was one of his pet subjects, and he also started making some plans for a new small family car.

After D-Day 1944, as light began to glimmer at the end of the long and tragic tunnel, Issigonis began work on his new machine in earnest. He had previously tried fitting independent front suspension to his Morris Ten, but this was completely unsuccessful, the weight distribution of the car being totally unsuited to the system. He came to the only sensible conclusion that it was not practical to try to work out new and better suspension layouts on existing vehicles; his new car, he reasoned, would give him an ideal opportunity to put his thoughts to the test.

The 1949 two-door Minor, with grille-mounted headlamps and split windscreen.

This is the Series II Minor of 1953, with the overhead-valve A series engine.

In opting for a new, small, economy car, the great designer was going out on something of a limb; many people thought that the end of the war would bring prosperity and that the days of the 'baby' car were numbered. He thought that petrol rationing would remain in force – as indeed it did – for many a year after peace returned, so that motorists would be able to buy nothing but frugal vehicles. Fortunately, the Nuffield Organisation took the idea seriously and the management agreed to Issigonis' request for the assistance of Jack Daniels, who had worked very closely with him on his suspension designs.

From the start, it was established that the new car would have unitary construction and independent front suspension. Precious little else was firmly fixed, however. At the outset, Issigonis decided to use a brand new horizontally opposed four-cylinder engine, mounted well forward in the nose of the car to give a forward weight bias; this unit had the same configuration as that of the rival Volkswagen, but in this case the power plant made use of water as the cooling medium, rather than air. Two capacities were to be available – 800cc and 1000cc – and side valves were to be fitted. A three-speed gearbox and independent

rear suspension were to accompany the novel engine, torsion bars providing the suspension medium at all four corners. Front-wheel drive was even considered.

Several prototypes of the new car were built to this specification, under the code name Mosquito, but there was simply neither the time nor the money to develop all these concepts sufficiently and to tool-up to make them. In those prototype stages, the body was the same width as that of the old Morris Eight, which this machine was to replace, but Issigonis did not think that the proportions were right. He puzzled long and hard about what exactly was wrong with the shape, but he could not come up with the exact answer. He was fairly sure that the problem lay in the width, so he asked the mechanics to cut a car in half longitudinally : he then stood well back and watched as they moved the two halves apart – and suddenly everything looked just right. The difference in width was only 10 cm (4 in), but it appeared to be far greater. Like the rest of the

The wood-clad estate car was announced in 1953.
It looked very smart but was difficult to maintain.

vehicle, the body of the new Minor was the work of Issigonis; it is likely that he was influenced at the time by the curvy nature of current American cars – whatever the case, the body was seen as exceptionally stylish.

When the Minor, known additionally as the Series MM, was finally announced in October 1948, Issigonis had been forced by lack of time to dilute many of his bold ideas. Nevertheless, his new car created a storm and took Morris into a whole new era.

Gone was the flat-four, replaced by the more ordinary unit from the Series E Morris Eight. However, this was no bad engine, being an in-line side-valve four producing $27\frac{1}{2}$ bhp from its 918cc. Gone, too, was the idea of front-wheel drive: the engine drove the rear wheels through a single-dry-plate clutch and a four-speed gearbox, with synchromesh on the upper three ratios. The central gear lever was of the long 'pudding-stirrer' variety, requiring large movements between gears. An open propeller shaft transferred the motion to a live rear axle, all thoughts of independent rear suspension having been forgotten, and this contained a hypoid-bevel final-drive unit.

Front suspension, which did remain independent, was by lower wishbones acting on longitudinal torsion bars; lever-type hydraulic dampers provided the upper links. At the rear, the live axle was located by semi-elliptic leaf springs and again lever-type hydraulic dampers smoothed the ride.

Steering gear consisted of a rack-and-pinion unit and the four-wheel brakes were hydraulically operated. Two body styles were originally available, a two-door saloon and a two-door tourer, both with four seats.

With a maximum speed of around 105 km/h (65 mph) and fuel economy 7l/100 km (40 mpg) or so, the Minor immediately caught the public eye. It had much more than that to offer, however; it was totally practical, with plenty of room and good visibility, and it handled much better than had any similar car before. It was easy to drive and a remarkably safe car.

One unusual aspect of the design was that the headlamps were mounted in the radiator grille;

this left the wings uncluttered and gave the whole body a very smooth shape. Unfortunately, American regulations, and rumours that Europe was about to follow suit, forced Morris to raise the lamps to a minimum of 0.6 m (2 ft) from the ground, and this necessitated fairing them into the wings. This change took place first on a newly introduced four-door model in late 1950, but the new arrangement was standardised in January of 1951.

The price of the original car was low enough for the Morris Minor to sell extremely rapidly. Changes during its long and healthy life were legion. Apart from the moving of the headlamps, the first major modification came at the end of 1952, when the merger of Austin and Morris to form the British Motor Corporation enabled Morris to adopt Austin's 803cc overhead-valve A series engine, as used in the A30. Although it was smaller, this unit produced more power, at 30 bhp, so performance was not lost. The four-door was changed before the two-door cars, but the latter followed suit in February of 1953. Later in the year, van, pick-up and traveller versions followed; the commercials were interesting in that they were given a box-section chassis to cope with extra payload. The new engine brought the designation Series II.

By the end of 1956, nearly $\frac{1}{2}$ million Minors had left the Cowley production line, and the engine was again changed. This time it was enlarged to 948cc, which took power output to 37 bhp and top speed over 112 km/h (70 mph) for the first time. Now known as the Minor 1000, the Morris also gained other improvements, including a larger rear window, a one-piece curved windscreen and a remote-control gearchange. Flashing indicators were introduced in 1961, but by far the most important event of that year was that, on 4 January, the 1 millionth Morris Minor was built.

To celebrate this event, the company made 350 Minors in a special lilac paint finish (which was particularly unpleasant) and adorned them with badges proclaiming that they were Morris

The convertible tourer was always one of the more popular versions and had become a valuable rarity by the 1980s.

1 000 000s. These were used by dealers for a publicity campaign and were eventually sold to the public.

In the following year, the engine's capacity was enlarged once more, this time to 1098cc, and power went up to 48 bhp. Fuel consumption had by now dropped to nearly 9.4 l/100 km (30 mpg), but the performance of the car was more lively than it had previously been. To enhance this effect, a new gearbox with baulk-ring synchromesh was installed at the same time. This was much more efficient and much longer lasting than its cone-type predecessor.

This was the last major mechanical change to the Morris Minor, which had become so dear to so many hearts. A great many more detailed alterations did subsequently take place, but the car was good enough as it was to soldier on into the 1970s. It was finally replaced in 1971 by the Morris Marina, which shared some of the Minor's components. To most people who knew anything about Minors this was a mistake; with over $1\frac{1}{2}$ million Minors under their belt, the British Leyland managers needed a really special car to follow on, and it was doubtful whether they had found it. Maybe even they lived to regret their decision to drop this stalwart when they did.

AUSTIN A30/35

Towards the end of the 1940s, it was becoming clear that Austin and Morris were beginning to cut each other's throats, particularly in export markets, where the sales of both marques were losing ground. The idea of a merger between the two major concerns had first been mooted as early as 1924, and had been favoured by Herbert Austin; however, on that occasion, William Morris was against the scheme, even though such a combination would have left his own concern as the senior partner.

By 1950, affairs were somewhat different, Morris being much weaker than it had been nearly 30 years previously. Even so, Leonard Lord, by then in charge of Austin, and Lord Nuffield (Morris had been elevated to the peerage) recognised the fact that the two giants could operate much more efficiently as a team than as rivals. It seemed that a merger would be finalised very quickly when the two men agreed terms, but they had reckoned without their respective colleagues, particularly Morris's Chief Executive, Reginald Hanks.

It was probably the delay caused by this disagreement that allowed Austin's new baby car, the A30, to come into being at all. After all,

Morris had announced the remarkable Minor in 1948 and there would be no sense in having two cars of a similar class within the same group. As things were, Lord soon made it clear to the Morris Board that his company fully intended to proceed with plans for the new car. Of course, it is now well known history that the merger did finally take place, in 1952, and the British Motor Corporation (BMC) was born, but by then the A30 was 1 year old.

The new car was really the latest in the line of Austin Sevens, despite its A30 name. It was just about all new and was especially important because it was the first car from Longbridge to dispense with the traditional chassis and replace it with a unitary construction body.

The engine was equally new. It was a four-cylinder, water-cooled unit, of 803cc, with pushrod-operated overhead valves and a power output of 28 bhp in this, its Zenith-carburettored form. (The most remarkable feature about this conventional power unit, known as the A series

The A30 was quite successful in competition. Here one competes in the 1953 Land's End Trial.

engine, is that it was still in use in 1981, in only slightly modified form and in various capacities, in such cars as the Mini and the Allegro.)

A single-dry-plate clutch connected the front-mounted motor to a four-speed gearbox, with synchromesh on first, second and third gears, and with a long, flimsy gear lever. From there, an open propeller shaft drove the rear axle by means of a hypoid final drive and a differential.

Independent front suspension was fitted, which operated through wishbones and coil springs, while, at the rear, quarter-elliptic leaf springs looked after the location of the live rear axle. Hydraulic lever-arm dampers were fitted all round.

Rack-and-pinion steering was the norm, while braking was looked after by hydraulic units on all four wheels. The handbrake operated, by cable, on the rear wheels.

When it was announced in 1951, the A30 attracted considerable interest from the public, for it promised to be nimble, practical and economical. What is more the body was very stylish, even if very small, and bore all the trademarks of its Austin parentage. Indeed, the A30 was respectably quick; it could reach 80 km/h (50 mph) in under 30 seconds, which may seem extremely slow by today's standards, and it had a maximum speed of over 97 km/h (60 mph). It was also very frugal, managing well over 7 1/100 km (40 mpg), something which reflected its low overall weight of only 660 kg (13 cwt). It had always been Austin policy to price their products just below their Morris rivals; the A30 should have cost more than the Morris Minor, but it was actually fractionally cheaper.

The A30's biggest drawback lay in its handling; it instilled very little confidence in its driver and was unstable to the point where there were many cases of cars overturning on corners. This was a fact which certainly let the little Austin down when it came to competing with the Morris Minor, which by now was selling in enormous quantities. One of its saving graces, however, was its record of reliability, although this was obviously something which was built up, rather

The four-door A30 of 1953; a good engine was let down by indifferent handling.

The A35 replaced the A30 in 1956. The most obvious external difference was the large rear window.

than being an immediate plus point. The engine of the A30 was so good, in fact, that one of the first changes to take place in BMC after the merger was to install the Austin A series engine in the Morris Minor, in place of its side-valve unit.

Modifications to the A30 did not come thick and fast; it sold well enough not to need them. However, 1954 saw a change in final-drive ratio from 5.125 to 4.875:1, which endowed the car with more relaxed cruising ability. Despite the car's poor reputation for handling, it had a great deal of potential and 'breathed on' by specialists it saw considerable success on the race tracks.

The most important change to the model came in 1956, when it was redesignated the A35. This had a larger rear window, a different grille,

flashing indicators and, most significantly, a larger engine, a 948cc version producing 34 bhp, which also found its way into the Morris Minor. The A35 had a maximum speed of over 112 km/h (70 mph) and still used very little fuel. In short, it was a far better car than the A30.

Sales continued to boom, but the car could never quite catch up with its Morris stablemate and, in 1962, it finally disappeared from the catalogues.

SIMCA ARONDE

The Simca company was set up in 1934, by a man called Henri-Theodore Pigozzi, with the sole aim of manufacturing Fiats under licence for the French market. The name, incidentally, was taken from the initials of the concern: Société Industrielle de Mécanique et Carrosserie Automobile. For the next 16 years, the company adhered faithfully to its original purpose in life and made nothing but re-badged versions of Italy's famous products; there were plenty of them, but there was nothing original about any of them. The longest lived and most famous were the Cinq, which was a French equivalent of the much revered 500 'Topolino', and the Huit, Simca's 508C Millecento.

These models, along with several others, were very successful, but by the end of the 1940s, Simca's designers were itching to produce their own car with an identity unique to it. There solution was quietly to get on and produce such a machine, so that it was not until the prototype was finished in early 1951 that the project was put to the organisation's senior management. The car was tentatively called the Neuf, or 9, and it was fortunate that the board actually liked it and gave it the go-ahead. However, they decided that it would not be known by a number, but that it would have its own special name; after a great deal of argument, or discussion, the name Aronde was agreed. The significance of this was that Simca's symbol then was a swallow and

The Simca Aronde went into production in October of 1951 and this was one of the first cars produced.

aronde was an old French word describing such a bird.

Although the engine was based on that used for so many years in the Simca Huit, the Aronde was a completely new vehicle, which owed no debt to any Fiats, or indeed the products of any other manufacturer. The body and chassis were of unitary construction, which made the car sturdy and torsionally stiff while it remained simple to construct. The 1221 cc engine was mounted at the front in the conventional longitudinal position and was a four-cylinder unit with a cast-iron block and an aluminium alloy cylinder head. The crankshaft was carried in three bearings beneath the in-line cylinders and the unit was water-cooled. The overhead valves were operated through pushrods and rockers by a single camshaft mounted at the side of the cylinder block.

From the engine, a single-dry-plate clutch formed the link to a three-speed, synchromesh gearbox, mounted in unit with the engine. An open propeller shaft transmitted the drive from there back to a live rear axle by way of a final-drive unit with hypoid-bevel gears, something which was a rarity in the early 1950s – most other cars used spiral-bevel gears, which were neither as efficient nor as hardy as these.

Front suspension, too, was very modern, with coil-spring/damper units and double wishbones, a system which has since become one of the most popular for front ends. At the rear, the springing was more conventional, with leaf springs locating the axle. Braking was taken care of by hydraulically operated drums all round, the hand-brake lever working the rear brakes mechanically.

Considering that the prototype was not shown until the beginning of 1951, it was something of a remarkable feat that the Aronde was introduced to the public in June of the same year. Unfortunately production could not get started until October, because the factory at Nanterre, on the Seine in Paris, had to be completely modernised and re-equipped. However, the customers do not seem to have minded waiting a few months, because people were clamouring to

In 1956, when this example was built, engine capacity was increased to 1290 cc.

The Aronde Oceane cabriolet of 1957, with Facel coachwork.

lay their hands on the first cars to leave the works.

Press reports were favourable, the car being respectably quick and nimble with its 45 bhp engine, and the immediate success of the Aronde took the company completely by surprise. The Simca Six had been dropped at the end of 1950, so the factory could turn all its attention to producing the Aronde and the Huit, which was the only other Simca still in the catalogues. The effort was obviously worthwhile, too, because 30 000 Arondes had been sold by the end of that first year, as against only 20 568 Huits. By the end of the following year nearly 70 000 Arondes had rolled off the production line and the old faithful Huit was finally dropped.

Apart from performing with suitable verve, the Aronde was extremely reliable and this was adequately demonstrated in 1953 when one example covered 100 000 km (62 139 miles) at an average speed of 100 km/h (62 mph); this was only one of many long distance records that were tackled and beaten by the Aronde around that time. Also in 1953, a 50 bhp sports version of the car was introduced, the first of a series of sports

coupés and convertibles which ran throughout the car's remaining life.

By 1954, six different versions of the Aronde were available, ranging from four-door saloons to the two-door convertible, and the coupé managed an extra 5 to 6 km/h (3 or 4 mph) over the more usual maximum of around 120 km/h (75 mph). Simca took over Ford France in 1954, which gave the company an extra, and more suitable, factory at Poissy. Production was then steadily shifted from Nanterre, until, by 1961, the old factory had been sold to Citroën.

A small capacity increase to 1290cc came in 1956, but this only raised the power output to 48 bhp, which made little difference to performance. More significant was the improvement in the sports engine, which was now turning out 57 bhp and was fitted not only to the coupés and convertibles, but to a new saloon variant known as the Montlhéry, which was capable of nearly

The Montlhéry was capable of nearly 145 km/h (90 mph) when it was introduced in 1956. This is the 1962 edition.

145 km/h (90 mph). In the following year, the standard engine found its way into a new model known as the Ariane 4. This was basically the old Ford Vedette V8 body, so the power unit provided the only link to the Aronde.

Of much greater significance in that year was the fact that Aronde production passed the $\frac{1}{2}$ million mark – and, what is more, demand showed no signs of tailing off. The company always kept abreast of public taste and need and in 1959 introduced a new 1090cc version of the car alongside the two 1290cc variants. This stimulated even greater demand and the magic 1 million figure was reached in February 1960.

In 1961 the engine was uprated again, with five bearings being incorporated, and the power output shot up, the sports versions having 62 bhp and later 70 bhp. Regardless of this, however, the Aronde was finally beginning to get a little tired and production was slowed down until the model was eventually dropped in 1964, over 12 years after its birth. This popular little car had by then won the hearts of over $1\frac{1}{2}$ million buyers and it was still very much in evidence for many years after on the roads of France and many other countries.

AUSTIN-HEALEY SPRITE/MG MIDGET

In the late 1950s, the British Motor Corporation (BMC) was doing very well with its sports cars: the MGA was being turned out by the thousand at Abingdon and the Healey 100-Six was keeping the workers highly occupied at Longbridge. The Healey connection had come about as a result of Donald Healey revealing his stylish new 100 model, powered by Austin's four-cylinder, 2660cc engine, at the London Motor Show of 1952. This attracted such a vast crowd, with its elegant, flowing lines and promise of sparkling performance, that Donald Healey quickly realised that his small company would never be able to manufacture enough cars to meet even a small part of the demand. This fact also occurred to Sir Leonard Lord, chief of Austin, who noticed the clamour around the stand. He and Healey came to an agreement whereby Austin would take over the manufacture of the new car, which would henceforth be known as the Austin-Healey 100, and Healey would play a part in new car development work and competition preparation.

Everything went according to plan, with the big Healey satisfying a great many sporting enthusiasts' desires. However, it was not very long before BMC, of which Austin had become part, decided that a small sports car would find an immediate large market. They set Donald Healey to work on the project, the brief being to design the car to use as many existing BMC components as possible.

Around this time, which was 1957, BMC undertook to move Austin-Healey from Longbridge to Abingdon, the traditional home of MG, which of course meant that all sports car production within the group would be in one place; Riley was moved out to free the necessary space. At the same time, a new design office was opened at Abingdon and this unit developed the basic scheme of Healey to suit the Corporation's own production requirements. Indeed, as more work was carried out, either at Longbridge or Abingdon, Donald Healey slowly faded from the scene.

The new Austin-Healey Sprite was unveiled in

By the time this Midget was made in 1974, the Sprite had been dropped.

May 1958 and was an instant success; as BMC had thought, it brought sports car motoring within the reach of thousands of people who had not been able to afford it before, with only cars in the league of the MGA or the big Healey to choose from. It represented remarkably good value and was particularly attractive, if a little unusual, with its headlights mounted in pods sticking up from the front of the bonnet. It was this feature which soon gave the little Sprite its now universally recognised nickname of 'Frog Eye'.

The vast majority of the mechanical parts were taken from other models in the BMC range, as had been specified, which is how the price could be kept low. The engine was a tuned version of the 948cc A series unit, as fitted then to the Morris Minor and the Austin A35. This three-bearing, four-cylinder motor had its power output raised from the A35's modest 34 bhp at 4750

The Mark I 'Frog Eye' Sprite, introduced in 1958. This one has the questionable luxury of a hard top.

rpm to a more respectable 42 bhp at 5000 rpm by dint of fitting tiny, twin SU carburettors and a slightly improved camshaft, which opened the overhead valves by means of pushrods and rockers. The A series engine had already been in use for 7 years, which probably made it seem fairly old even then, but incredibly it was still going strong in 1980, albeit with several different capacities, but nevertheless very much the same.

The single-dry-plate clutch and the four-speed gearbox, which were mounted in unit with the motor, were also standard A35/Minor components – even the gear ratios were unaltered. Synchromesh was fitted to second, third and top gears. An open propeller shaft transmitted the

drive to the standard A series live rear axle, which in this case housed a hypoid-bevel, final-drive unit with a ratio of 4.22 : 1.

Front suspension was by means of double wishbones and coil springs, while at the rear the axle was located by quarter-elliptic leaf springs and radius arms. Lever-type hydraulic dampers were fitted all round. Rack-and-pinion steering was standard and stopping was taken care of by drum brakes all round.

All this was mounted on a punt-type chassis, to which the all-steel body was welded. A two-door, two-seater convertible was the only style available, with rather cramped, draughty accommodation and a completely removable hood. The whole of the front end lifted up to give fairly good access to the engine, although it did not lift high enough to offer the legendary Triumph Herald/Spitfire space.

All in all, the Sprite was a primitive car offering

The MG equivalent of the Sprite appeared in 1961, together with the 1000 cc engine.

only the basics in creature comforts, but it had lively performance: with a maximum speed of over 129 km/h (80 mph), it handled well and it offered open air motoring for the young at heart.

The success of the Sprite prompted the MG men at Abingdon to think in terms of their own new small sportster. The BMC Mini had been announced in 1959 and its performance was such, particularly in terms of roadholding and handling, that it set new standards for sports cars. MG set about planning a two/four-seat, open-topped version of the Mini, using basically the same front end, and they got as far as building a prototype of this pretty little machine. However, the BMC overlords would not sanction the cost of tooling up to build such a car and decided

instead to concentrate on the Mini-Cooper. Judging by the success of the Cooper, and by the fact that Sir Alec Issigonis had remarked that the sports car was not very good, this may well have been the right decision.

This was in 1960 and it was then agreed to facelift the Sprite in order to give it a slightly more modern appearance and, at the same time, to introduce an MG equivalent of the car. The Mark II Sprite appeared in May 1961 with a boot, something which had been missing from the 'Frog Eye' (access was previously from behind the seats), and the headlights were conventionally mounted in the wings. A normal bonnet lid also replaced the opening front-end. Mechanically the Mark II was almost identical to the Frog Eye, but more power had been squeezed out of the engine by fitting a new camshaft, a new cylinder head, flat-topped pistons and slightly larger carburettors. New close-ratio gears, developed in competition, found their way into the gearbox.

The changes to the engine had added only about $4\frac{1}{2}$ bhp, but the car accelerated more quickly than before and its top speed was now nearly 145 km/h (90 mph). The MG version of the Sprite was announced a month later and revived the old Midget name, degrading it in the

The last version of the Austin-Healey Sprite was the Mk IV, announced in 1966 with a 1275 cc engine and a folding hood.

eyes of the faithful with this blatant piece of badge-engineering. For some unknown reason, the price of the MG was higher than that of the Austin Healey – there were no mechanical differences, perhaps the extra chromework was expensive – but, despite that, the Midget did manage to find a market and, strangely, has since always sold slightly better than the Sprite.

During this period, and for much of the 1960s, both Donald Healey and the BMC Competitions Department, itself based at Abingdon, were very active in preparing 'Spridgets', as they soon became known, for various types of competition. Probably the most famous examples, were the lightweight-bodied coupés built for long-distance sports car races, such as the Sebring 12-hour race; these were raced with great honour and soon became recognised as Sebring Sprites.

The London Motor Show of 1962 saw a new 1098cc version of the A series engine introduced for the Sprite and Midget, which also gained front disc brakes at the same time. With 55 bhp on tap at 5500 rpm, the little cars could now manage over 145 km/h (90 mph), with acceleration to match.

A far-more substantial change came in March 1964, when the Sprite became the Mark III and the Midget, the Mark II. The capacity remained at 1098cc, but the main bearings were enlarged and power was raised to 59 bhp by means of a new cylinder head. The line of the body was very subtly altered and it was equipped with a new curved windscreen; wind-up windows replaced sliding side-screens and exterior door handles were fitted for the first time. Handling was improved by the substitution of semi-elliptic rear springs in place of the old quarter-elliptic variety and the interior layout was changed by, among other things, the repositioning of the instrument panel. Wire wheels also became an optional extra. As saloon car performance caught up with that of sports cars, so the public was becoming less ready and willing to put up with a rough ride and spartan conditions as a necessary concomitant to sporting motoring. The new generation of Spridgets represented the first step in Abingdon's resignation to this fact and the truth of the matter was that the cars were much better for it.

The next stage came in 1966, when the London Motor Show cars were equipped with folding hoods in place of the awkward lift-off type with a separate frame. At the same time, the Mark IV Sprite and Mark III Midget acquired an even bigger engine, this time a 1275cc unit producing 65 bhp at 6000 rpm and once again raising the car's maximum speed, although this was still just short of the magic 'ton'. Rather ugly Rostyle wheels were offered soon after this, but the traditional wires could still be obtained by those who could be bothered to clean them.

In 1970, the agreement between BMC and Healey ran out, so at the beginning of 1971 the Sprite became the Austin Sprite. However, this change was shortlived, because, after only another 1000 cars had been assembled the Sprite was dropped altogether, the reason being that the MG was selling much better anyway. The 1971 Midget acquired a fuel tank of 32 litres instead of

American-regulation plastic bumpers grew at both ends of the 1975 Midget, which also gained a Triumph 1500 cc engine.

a miserly 27 (7 instead of 6 gallons), and the rear wheel arches were briefly altered to match the semi-circular front ones; this change was not popular and the styling soon reverted to type.

Still selling remarkably well, the Midget suffered the ultimate ignominy in 1975 (as far as MG purists are concerned) when it was made to share the new 1500cc power plant of its Leyland sister, the Spitfire. This Triumph unit was as long in the tooth as the A series, but a larger engine was needed to cope with US exhaust requirements and this unit was already available. In point of fact, the 66 bhp unit did the Midget no harm, at last taking its top speed over 161 km/h (100 mph) and making it an altogether brisker car. Far worse was the addition of Federal 8 km/h (5 mph) bumpers at both ends of the car: these black plastic monstrosities took away most of the Midget's character (as they had done with the ubiquitous MGB) and their worth – and indeed their necessity – was questionable.

Despite all this, and despite the fact that the Spitfire was a more practical car, with more room inside and better access, the BMC baby just soldiered on into the 1980s, finally being discontinued in February 1980, with over 300000 sales under its belt.

AUSTIN-MORRIS MINI

No one, not even designer (Sir) Alec Issigonis, could have forseen just how much the revolutionary Mini would change British lives when the car was announced in 1959. Apart from introducing a new household word to the language, the car cut across all class barriers so that it was as attractive to the high-powered city businessman as to the impecunious student and was ideal as a second car.

The concept of front-wheel drive was not new when Issigonis, who already had the design of the legendary Morris Minor to his name, sat down to plan his new baby car. However, its application in conjunction with a transverse in-line four-cylinder engine was totally original. Issigonis went further than this by adding a four-speed gearbox, with synchromesh on the upper three ratios, in unit with, and beneath, the engine, driven through an ingenious clutch arrangement by three primary gears. Final drive was by spur gears, no angle change being necessary, and drive shafts, with special constant-velocity universal joints, coupled the differential, which was bolted to the back of the gearbox, to the front wheels.

Perhaps the most remarkable aspect of this new Mini was the way in which every bit of space was so carefully used. The body was only 3 m (10 ft) long and yet there was ample room inside it for four adults and a small boot for luggage. The wheels were cleverly placed at the four corners of the body, so that they would not encroach on passenger space, but the effect of this, combined with the brilliantly simple rubber cone suspension, developed in conjunction with Alex Moulton, was to endow the new baby with astonishing cornering power and handling qualities.

The prototype Mini was equipped with the 948cc version of BMC's ubiquitous A series engine, but this made the car faster than was intended and an 848cc variety was substituted. It is interesting to note that, initially, the engine was fitted with the carburettor at the front, but various problems, such as carburettor icing and difficulty of access for servicing, prompted Issigonis to turn the whole unit round.

The 1000 cc Mini of 1978, externally little changed from the original of 1959.

The Mini was introduced in 1959 as the Austin Seven; like its namesake of 1922 it was intended to satisfy a need for a new type of small car. In this case, the Suez crisis of 1956 had produced a fuel shortage, but the only cars built for real economy were the bubble cars – the cyclecars of the 1950s. The Mini, as it very quickly became known, the title being a contraction of its Morris name, Mini Minor, was an economy car in all senses: it was small, it could manage 7 1/100 km (40 mpg) and it was cheap. This cheapness was achieved by offering only the bare essentials; for instance a heater was an optional extra, rubber mats covered the floor, door hinges were external, side windows slid and doors were opened from the inside by wire pulls.

The car was an immediate sales success, hitting the market in exactly the right place, and it was only a few months before younger owners began to discover the Mini's potential as a competition car. BMC fortunately recognised this sporting appeal, too, and offered the first of the Mini Coopers in October 1961. This had a 997cc

In the 1970s, all Mini estates gained the Clubman's extended front. This is a 1973 edition.

engine with twin carburettors, which boosted top speed from 112 km/h (70 mph) to over 129 km/h (80 mph). It also had disc brakes at the front and a remote-control gearchange in place of the standard 'pudding stirrer'. This Cooper was replaced in 1964 by a shorter-stroke 998cc-engined version with more effective disc brakes and sundry other modifications, but in the meantime the first of the S variants had been announced in March 1963. This was the 1071cc Cooper S, which, in addition to the special engine, had wider wheels and a brake servo, but which was short-lived, as it was superseded in the following year by two new Cooper S models, with 970cc and 1275cc engines. It was the 1275cc which really made its mark, continuing in production until 1971 and bringing BMC a great deal of competition success, including three Monte Carlo Rally wins (plus a fourth moral victory,

The Mark II Mini of 1967, outwardly distinguished by a new grille and rear lamps and an enlarged rear window.

the car being disqualified on a lighting technicality). Top speed of the 'standard' car approached 161 km/h (100 mph) and acceleration was astonishing.

All the Mini types have been steadily developed since 1959, the first major change being the introduction of hydrolastic suspension, borrowed from the larger 1100cc, in 1964. A Mark II Mini was announced in 1967 and was distinguishable by a larger rear window, new rear lights and a new grille. A 998cc engine was offered as an option on this car, giving slightly better performance and – more importantly – more relaxed cruising from a higher final drive ratio.

1971 saw a third Mark, which involved winding windows and concealed hinges, among other things; there was also a version with revised frontal bodywork alongside this, known as the Clubman. There was no 850cc Clubman, the standard engine being the 998cc, but a new

There were various models of Mini Cooper; this is the 998 cc version announced in 1964.

1275cc engine could also be had in this body, although this was by no means a replacement for the much more sporting and much mourned Cooper S.

Various other types of Mini have been produced during its life, including long-tailed, fairly luxurious Riley Elf and Wolseley Hornet variants, estate cars, with or without wood trim, a van, a pick-up truck and a Jeep-type utility vehicle known as the Mini-Moke. It was hoped that the Moke would attract military orders, but these did not materialise so the venture was not a profitable one.

The Mini continues into the 1980s very much modified since its introduction and no longer the austere runabout that it was, but it has never lost its character. Once again equipped with the old

The Mini Super of 1961 had various distinguishing features, such as bumper over-riders and chrome window trim.

rubber suspension its handling is as good as ever and it still uses very little fuel. It now has a gearbox which is pleasant to use, seats which are fairly comfortable and brakes which stop it and it still appeals to the same wide cross-section of the motoring public as it did in 1959.

Countless specials have been built around Mini components and several coachbuilders have exercised their art to turn Minis into extravagent playthings of the rich. Most manufacturers have copied Sir Alec Issigonis's brilliant front-wheel-drive layout, but none has actually produced a car of this size, all the others being of 'supermini' dimensions. Over $4\frac{1}{2}$ million Minis had been sold by 1980, which made it the best-selling British car of all time. Strangely, however, it has never been a real commercial success, being sold too cheaply in its early days; nevertheless it remains a totally practical car – a car for all seasons.

RENAULT 4

The idea for a brand new type of Renault came to the President of the company, Pierre Dreyfus, as a result of launching their first front-wheel-drive vehicle, the Estafette. The enormously successful 4CV had been in production since 1947 and had, by the end of the 1950s, made motoring an everyday possibility for over 1 million people; however, it was becoming somewhat old-fashioned and it was time for a change.

Dreyfus reckoned that French families were becoming more and more motoring orientated, with extra money to spend, and he realised that they were wanting to make even longer journeys, which in turn required larger, and more comfortable, interiors for small cars. The 4CV could not meet these new demands and in any case Dreyfus was already planning a whole new range of Renaults and he wanted the 4CV's successor to be the first of these.

He conceived a car which could be all things to all men; his idea was that the new baby would break down all class barriers and would be treated as a purely practical workhorse – in trying to explain his ideas to a somewhat dubious design team, he used the fashion analogy of a pair of denims, calling it the 'Blue Jeans' car.

The new car was given the project number 112 and preliminary design studies were put in hand in 1956. A long list of specifications was laid down by the Board and it was up to the designers to include every feature without pushing the price above a very meagre figure. Accessibility had to be good and internal dimensions had to be as large as possible in a car with a very small outward size. It had to be able to cope with all types of terrain and it had to have suspension capable of coping adequately with rough ground without shaking the passengers about unduly. The cooling system had to be able to work efficiently at unreasonable extremes of temperature and there were to be no grease points on the chassis. Performance had to be such that the car would have a maximum speed of around 112 km/h (70 mph), with lively acceleration to match, but that it would also use very little fuel.

When this Renault 4 was produced in 1975, the model was well on its way to 5 million sales.

In some areas, these rigid parameters left the design team very little room for manoeuvre. It was decided that, in order to have the best access, the car would be given five doors; this in turn meant that in order to offer the maximum possible interior space, it would be no use staying faithful to the 4CV's concept of a rear-mounted engine/trans-axle assembly, which demanded a rather high rear floor. The answer to this was to give the new machine front-wheel drive, so that there would be no need for even a propeller shaft tunnel.

Ground clearance was set at about 15 cm (6 in), in order to manage rough ground, and it was reckoned that all the other conditions could be met without too much expense. Prototypes were then built, and these were tested extensively over tens of thousands of miles, on test tracks and on roads, to make sure that the new vehicle would live up to the requirements of its progenitor.

Various commercial versions of the Renault 4 have been made; this is a 1980 457 kg (9 cwt) van.

Dreyfus even went to Sardinia to drive one of the test cars himself; he was so confident in the handling of the new machine that he went just a little too fast on a mountain road, disappeared over the edge and nearly put paid to himself and to the young engineer who was accompanying him.

The tests were successful, despite this setback, and the new Renault 4 was ready for the public by 1961. Unlike the 4CV, the new car had reverted to a separate chassis, but this gave great ease of maintenance, since most of the panels were bolted on, rather than welded on, and yet it was very light, at just over 560 kg (11 cwt). With its fifth door, the car amounted to a semi-estate and offered plenty of room for luggage, being tall.

The Renault 4 GTL of 1980 had an 1100 cc engine and could manage nearly 129 km/h (80 mph).

It had originally been intended to design an all-new engine for the latest Renault, but costs involved in an exercise like this made it much more sensible to make use of the fine little four-cylinder unit from the 4CV, which had been so thoroughly proven and was recognised as being flexible and lively, with plenty of low-speed torque. In its original form, this water-cooled, overhead-valve unit had a capacity of 747cc, although there was an R3 version which was smaller at 603cc. As in the 4CV, the clutch, gearbox and final drive were mounted in unit with the engine, only this time the whole assembly resided at the front. The engine was mounted behind the gearbox, with the clutch and final drive in between (drive from engine to gearbox passed over the final drive). A single-dry-plate clutch was installed and the gearbox had four forward ratios; the final drive comprised hypoid-bevel gears – for the first time in a

Renault and the front wheels were driven by way of double-jointed drive shafts.

The strangest thing about the transmission was the gearchange mechanism. This consisted of a rod which ran backwards from the gearbox, past the engine and through the bulkhead into the cockpit, where it protruded from the centre of the dash and was formed into a lever. Changing gear involved the driver in a series of push/pull and twist actions and it took even an experienced person some time to master the art.

Suspension was soft, yet comfortable, and it relied on longitudinal torsion bars at the front and transverse ones at the rear, with telescopic hydraulic dampers all round. The necessity for the torsion bars to overlap at the rear meant that the wheelbase was slightly longer on one side than on the other, although this was not noticeable, either visually or on the road.

Steering was by rack-and-pinion, while hydraulic drum brakes were fitted on all four wheels, with a mechanical handbrake operating only on the rear drums.

The little machine was as successful as Dreyfus had hoped. Its launch was delayed only a little by the necessity to retool the factory at Ile Seguin. On 6 July 1961, the last Renault 4CV left the production line and, almost immediately afterwards, practically the whole of the Renault workforce took its annual holiday. Only a few key figures stayed in order to supervise the dismantling of the old lines and the installation of the new. Within a month, the first production Renault 4 had been rolled out. Despite the fact that a short pre-production series had been manufactured previously, the 4 was not announced to the public until 4 October, 2 months after the factory reopened. However, straight away, vehicles were available for the public to drive and orders began to flood in.

As had been specified, the little Renault could manage nearly 112 km/h (70 mph), and it provided a perfect runabout for the average family. Nobody seemed to mind the fact that the car rolled almost right over on corners and pitched like a rocking horse under braking; it functioned extremely well (despite looking dangerous to the outsider it actually exerted a tenacious grip on the road which it would not relinquish easily). Not only did the 4 appear to

function well, it did so reliably; even when it did go wrong, repairs were simple, it being possible to change the cylinder liners, pistons and crankshaft bearings without removing the engine from the car. There was not even a problem about checking the coolant level regularly, as this was the first motor car to make use of a sealed cooling system.

In 1962, the R3 version was dropped, leaving a 750cc model for the home market and an 845cc export version, which was subsequently standardised. This produced 32 bhp at 4700 rpm and gave the car a top speed of 111 km/h (69 mph). Sales continued to gain momentum, so that, in February 1966, the 1 millionth car was made, which meant that it was selling faster than any other front-wheel-drive car – including the famous Mini.

Many other changes have come and gone since the Renault 4 first appeared, probably the most important being the incorporation of a new gearbox, from the Renault 5, in 1973, which had a more conventional gearchange, and the addition to the range of an 1108cc GTL version in 1980, with slightly more power and a maximum of 112 km/h (76 mph).

The sales record of the 4 has been astounding: September 1977 saw the 5 millionth example manufactured, which represented a record for a French car and is a very rare figure for any manufacturer to achieve. In 1980, there were still no signs of demand abating and nearly 6 million had been made. Pierre Dreyfus was obviously exactly right with his market analysis.

INDEX

Figures in **bold** refer to colour illustrations and those in *italic* to black and white illustrations.